THE BIG
BLACK BOOK

**WALLACE
FAIRFAX**

Backbeat
Books

An Imprint of Hal Leonard LLC

CONTENTS

INTRODUCTION

Spinal Tap are the greatest band that have ever existed. Bigger than Def Leppard, braver than Bon Jovi, and even more popular in Sweden than Europe (in 1979). Spinal Tap are better than all of those bands combined, times ten – and then multiplied by a million. The numbers don't lie.

There's no need to fact check that statement either, or Google it, or Ask Jeeves, or whatever you people do to learn things these days. You just have to believe me because I have no reason to lie to you just to validate the years of devotion I have poured into this group.

Yes, when it comes to metal done heavy and loud all you need is Hubbins, Tufnel and Smalls ... and Shrimpton, Savage, Pepys, Childs, Pudding, etc.

Over their 16 studio albums and dozens of what critics cruelly called "unnecessary" singles, Spinal Tap have built a legacy that will continue far into the future when our robot overlords require our souls for batteries, a future that may not contain any new Tufnel, St Hubbins and Smalls compositions, but thankfully the highly prolific tapestry of music they have bequeathed us to this day will not leave us yearning for any more. We've got enough.

Spinal Tap are survivors. They are innovators. They are loud revolutionaries who seek only rock and rock salvation.

When it comes to touring the world and elsewhere, Spinal Tap have been there, done that and bought the tight-fitting Spandex t-shirt to prove it.

This Big Black Book you're holding isn't just a book – I mean, obviously, it *is* just a book, it can't do your tax returns, for example – but it's also more than that. It's an education. It's a deep dive into a cherished moment in time when all that mattered was a filthy power chord progression, lyrical innuendo and unwashed long hair that had been shampooed by the gods of metal and conditioned by the angels of mercy. If you had all these things on your tour bus – and you really did need nothing else back then – then you were guaranteed AAA immortality in the backstage pantheon of the Rock and Roll Hall of Fame.

There is no magic formula to Spinal Tap. They're just regular guys with great hair, great attitude and great songs you can bang your head to – not too fast, and not too slow, just right. Yes, Spinal Tap are the Goldilocks of rock…and that pretty much sums up how I feel about them in the word count I was told I needed to fill for this page.

So, before we begin this adventure into the only history of rock 'n' roll you'll ever need to read, get your devil horns at the ready[*], turn your lusty adoration up to 11, put on your favourite Tap album and take your hearing aids out because it's time to rock out with England's loudest band… SPINAL TAP!

Wallace Fairfax, Clitheroe, 2017

[*] Be warned, this will make turning the pages very difficult.

"But hey, enough of my yakkin'. What do you say, let's boogie!"

Opposite: *"It's more like going, going to a, a national park or something. And there's, you know, they preserve the moose. And that's, that's my childhood up there on stage. That moose, you know."*
Derek Smalls

**"YOU WANT IT, RIGHT?
DIRECT FROM HELL: SPINAL TAP!"**

THE EARLY YEARS

Friends since the age of eight, growing up next to each other on Squatney Road, and singing to each other all the way home from school, David and Nigel never could have imagined that only a few short years later they would form a group(s) that would eventually make their dreams come true. But before they found global fame all over Europe and North America as Spinal Tap, they first had to find global fame on the rough streets of East London…

"We were not university material," David St Hubbins admitted to Marty DiBergi for the filming of "rockumentary" *This Is Spinal Tap*, referring to his and Nigel's limited experience (and understanding) of education, a by-product of their poor upbringing in East London's least-educated neighbourhood, Squatney (rebranded in 2008 as Squatney-near-Thames). While this was news to Nigel at the time, the two boys knew, deep down, that for them it was rock 'n' roll … or bust. But not the good kind of bust. The other kind.

However, before Nigel and David formed the Thamesmen in 1965, the two fledgling teenage singer-songwriters were both occupied in their own, separate bands following a falling-out over a girl both boys fancied. The girl didn't want to be named in this book, so let's call her Jane. Once the two playground suitors found out that Jane found both David and Nigel to be "repellent," the two boys kissed and made up (not literally), but by that point they were fronting their own groups. Nigel was in the Lovely Lads, a skiffle band (they were all the rage back then), though as Nigel remembered, "We were more of a scuffle band, as we'd bash heads in if people didn't applaud us." After learning to play the acoustic guitar a year

earlier, even though he had asked his parents for a concert grand piano, a bassoon and a harp, which they simply could not afford, Nigel realized he needed a louder outlet for his curry-themed songs. David, a burgeoning Squatney songwriter, who had been selling songs for food since he was 11, was leading the Creatures to relative obscurity. In 1964, when both bands split up, David and Nigel bottled up their petty differences (resentments that would later erupt in 1982) and began performing as the Originals, jamming together again outside London's poshest Tube stations. However, another local East End band had already secured the name the Originals, and were bigger in size than Nigel and David, so the non-original Originals were forced to change their name to the New Originals, before becoming the Regulars, while the original Originals then changed their name to the Regulars, leaving the Originals name free for the non-original Originals (now called the Regulars). "We could go back to the Originals, but what's the point?" said David St Hubbins. It was a confusing time.

In August '64, as the New Originals, first jammed with drummer John 'Stumpy' Pepys, then a member of the Leslie Cheswick Soul Explosion, in the upstairs of their local Squatney pub, the Bucket (then the Bucket

---

"The Regulars – they changed their name back to the Regulars and we thought well, we could go back to the Originals, but what's the point?"

Nigel Tufnel

"Well, there was another group in the East End called the Originals and we had to rename ourselves."

Nigel Tufnel

and Pail, now Shoo). David and Nigel were never happy with the New Originals name, so changed it to the Regulars, shortly before they disbanded the whole group when the trio received an invite to go on a mini-tour with the Johnny Goodshow Revue. It was on this fateful tour (a disaster by all accounts) that the three teenagers met ex-Cheap Dates bassist Ronnie Pudding, and at the end of Revue tour, the foursome decided to become one. "We became the Thamesmen at that point," Nigel remembered, though only just.

Above: *The Bucket, the pub where the band first rehearsed. It is now an upmarket patisserie for hipsters, called Shoo.*

THE THAMESMEN

Following the confusion that arose from calling themselves the Originals, the newly formed pre-Tap Thamesmen (pronounced "Temsmen") finally had a great name and were sticking with it forever, except for when they briefly changed it to the Dutchmen and before permanently replacing it in 1966 with Spinal Tap. With a record deal with Abbey Records (agreed verbally with no support contractual paperwork in place), the Thamesmen had begun to sniff the first smells of success.

The Thamesmen period of 1965-66 proved to be David and Nigel's most successful era, with 'Cup and Cakes' bringing home the bacon with its double A-side partner, the sneering, cash-themed 'Gimme Some Money.' The songs' chart success was down largely to the fact that they both sounded incredibly similar to hits recorded by the Beatles, a well-known Liverpudlian foursome who had become increasingly well-known for making lots of money.

'Cups and Cakes,' with its simple, and sickly sweet, lyrics asking the listener to share 'tea and cake' with the band, was a song that, for once, wasn't about curry, the source of inspiration for (too) many of Nigel's earliest tracks. On the flipside of the single was 'Gimme Some

Money' a composistion that highlighted David and Nigel's deep desire for becoming rich, a dream that they would often talk about as poor Squatney rascals while sharing deep-fried cotton wool balls, the only nutrition their families could afford. The two singles portrayed the two opposing (bipolar) sides of Spinal Tap's lead songwriters, a split personality that would inform and define much of their output, from aggressive, sex-obsessed innuendos ('Sex Farm') to tender, sex-obsessed innuendos ('Lick My Love Pump').

With 'Cups and Cakes' / 'Gimme Some Money' riding high up the backside of the UK and US charts, the band were invited to play, for the first and only time, on the national treasure of British TV, the light entertainment show, *Pop, Look & Listen* in July 1965. They performed 'Gimme Some Money.' With "the Peeper" Joe "Stumpy" Pepys and Ronnie Pudding kneeding and dusting the rhythm section, the Thamesmen's "British-invasion" sound was hitting all the right notes with the screaming "teenage" people that had suddenly become ever so popular everywhere.

Following this TV appearance, the Thamesmen began doing something they would make a career out of: touring. The band, flushed with cash from the dual-singles' success, and feeling reckless, put together a Benelux Nations (Belgium, the Netherlands and Luxembourg) Tour with a then 16-year-old keyboardist Jan van der Kvelk, someone they had befriended at Amsterdam's notorious Long-Hair Club. For the Thamesmen, the Benelux nations tour was a no-brainer. "If you trace the old blues that came from Chicago and Mississippi and New Orleans – you trace that back across the Atlantic to Africa. And then from Africa it goes back to, I guess, Belgium," said David of their strategic touring decision. The Benelux gigs even briefly

prompted the group to change their name to the Dutchmen, hoping it would spur further success across the three nations. It didn't.

In August 1966, David, Nigel, Pepys, Pudding and British keyboardist Denny Upham travelled by aeroplane for the first time – and in Upham's case, the only time – across the Atlantic Ocean to New York, USA. After a few days of getting stiff necks from a lot of looking up, the band performed their first US show at the Electric Banana in Greenwich, Manhattan. In the audience on this fateful night was one of Tap's biggest fans, a "teenager" called Marty DiBergi, the man who would ultimately ruin the band for everyone else, following the VHS success of *This Is Spinal Tap* in 1984. The Electric Banana gig would remain the one-and-only US show the Thamesmen would ever play. Their next gig, at London's Music Membrane three months later in December 1966, would see the first incarnation of Spinal Tap rise out of the Thamesmen' ashes, starting a fire that would burn with patchy levels of success for the next four decades.

Opposite: *Brothers by other mothers, Nigel and David.*

THAMESMEN PLAYERS

TONY BRIXTON (keyboards) 1965–66

JIMMY ADAMS (the horn) 1965–66

LHASA APSO (vocals) 1965–66

GEOFF CLOVINGTON (the horn) 1965–66

SCHINDLER, LITTLE DANNY (harmonica, vocals) 1965–66

TAP UP CLOSE:
DAVID ST HUBBINS

David St Hubbins is the heart and soul of Spinal Tap. And the legs. And, possibly, the arms, but don't tell Derek. As the band's lead singer and (quieter) lead guitarist, it is David's role to write songs with pleasurable moments, i.e. the bridges, to counteract Nigel's more dramatic musical follies. David is the blonde to Nigel's brunette, the pork to his sweet potatoes.

David was born at Squatney Women's Hospital on August 13, 1943 (a year older than brother-from-another-mother, Nigel), at the tender womb age of ten months old. "He loved it in there," said David's mother, Davina, who went through a marathon 55-hour labour just to get the bulky 11lb infant out. Doctors noticed David had actually tried to climb upwards into his mother's lungs, believing that was the right way out.

David has been called many things in his lifetime: "Lazier than a dead budgie," was Ronnie Pudding's biased (and lazy) clichéd opinion, "incompetent" said his dad, Ivor, a more talented musician than his son. But the names David was called at the Sulfur Hill Academy for Boys, where the bullies were "a rougher breed of gentility," have stuck with him for all his adult life. But, being a professional, he's never let it interfere with his work.

Growing up in Squatney, East London, a rough area in the '50s and '60s, but completely gentrified now, was another motivation. A bored teenager, lacking in a desire to participate educationally, David dreamed of leaving the squalor of Squatney behind. "Where is Squatney? Nowhere, really. Seriously. It's at sort of an obtuse angle to the right of Embankment and straight on till morning," he has said of his hometown. "Don't look for it on the map, it's not there. East London council took it off 'cos they were so ashamed of it. It was not a great tourist area and they figured people who lived there knew where it was, so why put it on the map?"

It wasn't until David was nine that he felt happy for the first time. It was when he met his future partner-in-pun, Nigel Tufnel. Nigel's family had moved next door to David's on Squatney Road, and their bedrooms conveniently faced each other. David's family lived in flat No.45, Nigel's lived next door at flat 47. They did not know each other at first but befriended one another when they realized they both attended St Scubbins Primary School and rather than walking to school alone (which was all the rage then) they would kick cans and roadkill down the street as they walked

"Here lies David St Hubbins... and why not."

David St Hubbins

to school. Their moneyless upbringing uniting them in their desire to break free of the shackles of poverty. But rather than get a proper job that paid the bills, they both yearned to be rock 'n' roll stars, arguably the most unstable, volatile, and unlikely career to obtain financial security, but common sense and logic did not factor into their dream. Despite not having any sex appeal (at the time) or any natural musical talent, the two boys would sit on their respective windowsills and talk for hours about living their lives on the road, playing their music to adoring fans. "We're closer than brothers," Nigel said of their long-lasting relationship in DiBergi's "rockumentary" *This Is Spinal Tap*. "Brothers always fight, have disagreements, and all that but we really have a relationship that's way, way, past that. We've grown up, but really we still feel like children much of the time, even when we're playing."

Between the ages of 13 and 14, Nigel and David began singing rhyming melodies to each other, "a sort of fun English lesson," David said. "We left school and started playing Tube station skiffle. It was like how iron filings feel about a magnet. We were the filings, Spinal Tap became the magnet," David would later claim, rather nonsensically.

David's life changed forever, for the better (?) when he found an acoustic guitar in a skip behind his parent's house. He was 12. As far as David was concerned, this wasn't Mrs Arnold from No.26 throwing away unwanted goods before moving to a new house, this was fate telling David to be a rock star. Technically it was theft, David's mum said, but no one from the local constabulary ever turned up at the door. "The guitar is the most portable of instruments, I think," David recalled of the moment. "With the exception of vocals, which are extremely portable also."

With the guitar always by his side, it wasn't long before Nigel and David's pre- (and post-) school song-singing turned into songwriting. And so it was, on December 14, 1961, the two boys recorded their first composition together at a studio that was conveniently, almost suspiciously, located at the end of Squatney Road, next to the neighbourhood's most run-down pub,

the Queen's Lips (previously called the Bun & Puffy and the Restless Cheese, now called The Gun).

The song was titled 'All the Way Home.' Written in a 12-bar blues framework, and reminiscent of David's blues idol, Blind Bubba Cheeks. "He was not legally blind, though, he was myopic," David has said poignantly of his first musical icon. 'All the Way Home' was not David's first stab at songwriting. In the late 1950s, specifically 1959, David, aged 16, sold some of his first original compositions to Blue World China, another Squatney-based skiffle band.

David and Nigel lost touch for a few months in their mid-teens, as most teenage boys do, trying to expand their friendship circles. David fell in with the design school set and Nigel befriended animals he would see in trees. They also formed different bands. "Well, before Spinal Tap, we were in different groups," recounted David. "I was in a group called the Creatures, which was a skiffle group and Nigel was in the Lovely Lads." When both bands dissolved amid a quagmire of "talent-based differences," the opportunity arose for David and Nigel to form the Originals. The rest is history. (Go back and re-read page 8 onwards.)

David's love has always been music, even after Tap broke up. He has never followed in the family's footsteps, literally, his ancestry is steeped in feet-based history, dating back to the eleventh century and Saint Hubbins, the Patron Saint of Quality Footwear. Even when Tap were on hiatus from 1988 to 1992, David kept his musical toes in the water to manage the art-rock group Lamé (previously Bumdummy, originally called Diaperload) leading them to little success but massive disappointment.

David has been married and divorced twice. He and Jeanine Pettibone divorced in early 2000, though they remain on friendly terms today, often visiting each other's houses to align their cosmic chakras and channel their zodiac spirit animals. David also has two sons, Misha, with Jeanine, and Jordan, from his first marriage to Pamela.

Jordan and Pamela declined to be interviewed for this book.

"It's an unusual name. Well, he was an unusual saint. He's not a very well-known saint."

David St Hubbins

David St Hubbins: *"He was the Patron Saint of Quality Footwear."*

"Don't it feel good, with the Thamesmen and 'Cups and Cakes.' The Thamesmen later changed their name to Spinal Tap and they had a couple of B-side hits. They are currently residing in the 'Where are they now' file."

DJ Johnny Q, 106FM

SPINAL TAP (1967)

(OR SPINAL TAP SINGS '(LISTEN TO THE) FLOWER PEOPLE' AND OTHER FAVOURITES)

The year 1967 was a decisive one for Tap's primary songwriters Tufnel and St Hubbins. Following two years lost in the LSD wilderness while performing as the Thamesmen, the duo decided they had to change everything about themselves if they wanted to become really famous. With a new band name and a newly installed Satanist bass player, things finally stopped going sideways. Now, the only direction they could travel was up. Or at the very least, a bit more to the left.

Having taken quite a bit of beating, and quite a lot of acid, since the heavy rotation of band personnel that defined the Year of Our Tap 1965, as well as the public failure of the Benelux Nations Tour (while performing under the name the Dutchmen), the Thamesmen were in need of some TLC and a cup of tea, and as Lady Luck would have it, this tender loving care arrived aptly during the "Summer of Love," 1967.

Before the band could continue forwards, and therefore upwards, however, the Thamesmen had to die a horrible death, metaphorically, but also literally. Towards the end of 1966, David and Nigel had been considering changing the band's name. They had taken the Thamesmen as far as they wanted to go, and it was time to tell them that their services were no longer required, even though they were the Thamesmen. They had to fire each other, and then re-employ themselves as the same people, but in a different band.

It was Tufnel, in a rare moment of lucidity during a particularly inspired, if heavy, acid trip that devised the band's new moniker – SPYNAL TAP. When

the band was choosing a name for the group, shortly before their first gig at London's Music Membrane in December '66, they had all considered a few options – Ravebreakers, Doppel Gang, Silver Service, Bisquits, Love Bisquits – names that had all been written down at one point but then lost to the Sands of Time, which was also one of the name suggestions.

When Tufnel suggested "Spynal Tape," he quickly agreed with himself that that was nonsense, and blurted out "Spynal Tap" instead. Upham, Pudding, St Hubbins and drummer John "Stumpy" Pepys, were all too out of it to care. Left to his own devices, Tufnel was initially going to spell the group's name SPYNAL TAP, to fit in with the mid-1960s trend for band names being misspelt – the Testycles and the Knuckles (pronounced *Ker-na-calls*) were then riding up the back of the charts – but settled on "Spinal Tap." As Smalls later explained, "We thought it's supposed to be s-p-y, but to be clever, Nigel called it s-p-i. We found out later that he had spelled it right by mistake."

So proud of their new name, the band became

convinced (despite much expert advice to the contrary) that it would make an effective album title. And so it was, in July 1967, Spinal Tap released *Spinal Tap*.

Sadly, their US label Megaphone was unconvinced by their new name – a Spinal Tap is a medical procedure in America, but known in the UK as a Lumbar Puncture, hence the band's unawareness – and decided to alter the title of the band's début album to *Spinal Tap Sings '(Listen to the) Flower People' and Other Favourites*, to highlight the sure-fire hit on the LP. The rest of the album was considered to be "mainly filler."

Written by Ronnie Pudding, '(Listen to the) Flower People' was well-received following their appearance on *Jamboree Bop* on American TV on July 3. The band's performance was the shot to the arm the fivesome desperately needed, following months of intense inactivity. Though some fans and critics questioned the authenticity of Tap's "psychedelic period" with many music magazines labelling it a "stunt" to ride on the coat-tails of the lingering, harmony-laden folk-pop scene created by fellow LSD-mongers Aztec Wizzards and NWA (Nice White Americans), the band were unfazed.

"Yes, that 'Flower People' bit was real," David reported to calm the swelling criticism. "We certainly did go through a psychedelic period. At least, I guess we did – it's all a bit unclear to me now. You'll have to understand that when I picture the year 1967 in my head, the '7' is sort of smeared and it just winds up…I kind of come out of the smear at '71. So, it's a bit of a blur to me."

Despite the new-found fame in America, good fortune did not linger long. 'Flower People's' writer, bassist Pudding, had reached breaking point. He wanted to write music, so the band fired him. "He knew how to make those little dots, he'd make these little sort of balloon things on this lined paper and everything, and link 'em together with little strings and all that, the whole bit," Nigel said. Pudding's talent for composition – rare for a bassist – caused friction with Tap's primary writers. They were "confused" by the idea that a bassist could write songs equal to theirs. "Oh yeah, I'd say there was screaming hatred at this point," recalled Nigel of his relationship with Pudding at the time.

Following Pudding's dismissal, the role of bassist fell to former art student and future divorcée, Derek Albion Smalls. With Smalls installed, and their recording of

TRACKLIST

1. **'(Listen to the) Flower People'**
2. **'Have a Nice Death'**
3. **'Bonjour Monsieur'**
4. **'Up The Bucket'**
5. **'Best To Forget'**
6. **'Backside'**
7. **'The Ballad of Roy G. Biv'**
8. **'Rhymes With Orange'**
9. **'You Caught My Eye With Both Hands'**
10. **'Last Train to Basildon'**
11. **'Dry Tears'**

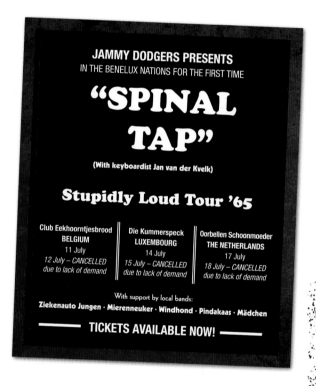

someone else's song in the charts, Spinal Tap's big break had finally broken them. "We had the world's ear," David remembers. "We were changing the world," agreed Derek. "We toured the world and elsewhere."

With Elsewhere calling, it was down to Spinal Tap to answer the phone. But who was going to pick it up?

Above: *Original poster for Spinal Tap's Benelux tour, 1965.*
Opposite: *The Thamesmen perform on* Jamboree Bop, *July 3, 1967.*

WE ARE ALL FLOWER PEOPLE (1968)

Released in 1968, Tap's "difficult second album" *We Are All Flower People* was considered to be no more difficult than the rest of the group's albums, which were all considered difficult. A labour of love for the band but a tough sell locally, regionally and internationally for Megaphone, who were beginning to question who exactly did Spinal Tap think they were, and more importantly, what on earth did they think they were doing?

Upon the release of *We Are All Flower People*, Megaphone A&R executive, Arnie Plimsole, remarked, "Sales, when they occurred, were disappointing." This disappointment was visible among the band, who expected the critical backlash from "the plebs" following the success of 1967's début, *Spinal Tap* ("People hate us because we're successful, that's the only reason," Nigel said), but still the group expected their fans to dig it, not bury it.

However, following *Spinal Tap*, a semi-successful album (commercially, if not critically) with a concept album about the life of Greek god Icarus, was an ambitious move by a band who had ignored their label's pleas to ditch the idea and release an album that people might "listen to." Unpersuaded by logic, Spinal Tap forged ahead with the writing, recording, re-writing, and re-recording, of an ambitious concept album. Derek, speaking about the record on the day of its release, was clear about the album's direction: "It was a very, very, early concept album about a man who decided, like Icarus, that he would put wings on and fly – but that he would be a jet airliner and that he would sell seats on himself to pay for the project. You know it was very acid-influenced." "Any metaphorical parallels should be avoided," observed one reviewer upon the album's release. "Unlike Icarus, Tap are still a long, long, way from having their moment in the sun."

With the album's lyrics and chord changes hitting a few bum notes with their teenage male audience, the album's chief songwriters Nigel and David decided they needed a scapegoat to blame for the album's failure to launch. Keyboardist Denny Upham was immediately dismissed. "The timing

TRACKLIST

1. 'We Are All Flower People'
2. 'To Fly'
3. 'I Have Wings'
4. 'I Am Flight'
5. 'Shouldn't Have Looked Down'
6. 'Get Me Away From the Ground'
7. 'Life is Looking Up'
8. 'The Incredible Flight of Icarus P. Anybody'
9. 'The Sun Burns'
10. 'Falling Without Wings'

is purely coincidental," said Nigel in a statement to the press, a day after the record's release. "We love Denny, but his subtle keyboard playing on the album is what made it unsuccessful. We asked him to turn it up, but he refused, so he had to go. We wish him well." With Upham on the slag heap (the same place Thamesmen keyboardists Tony Brixton, Nick Wax and Dicky

THE ELECTRIC BANANA

The Thamesmen
and
Hair Peace

HAPPY HOUR 6PM TO 6.30PM!
FREE CLOAKROOM FOR GIRLS' BAGS

TWO DRINKS FREE WITH THIS FLYER!
ALL YOU CAN EAT BUFFET!

Greenwich Village, New York --- January 15, 1966
Entry: $1.00

"It was really one of those things. The authorities said it's best to leave it unsolved." Nigel Tufnel

Laine had been sent in 1966), the band we were once again in disarray. Distraught by the album's frustrating sales, they turned to the prodigal talents of studio keys player, and devoted husband and father, Preston Billingham. Upham left big boots to fill, but Billingham was more than capable, having acquired prodigious musical skills through practice, hard work and natural talent, stuff the rest of Tap could only dream about. With Smalls' divorce currently distracting the bassist from songwriting, Nigel and David were unopposed when it came to anyone in the band matching their musical ability and songwriting. Billingham remained in the group for two days before quitting for "genuine family reasons." The band remained without keys until Viv Savage joined in 1975. The lack of keyboards in the band's line-up was a major factor in "turning up" the band's sound "to eleven" and acquiring bespoke amplifiers to deal with the additional wattage.

The year 1968 when the Vietnam War kicked off, was also the year the band "went electric," or as Tufnel described it, "went mental" ("sentimental metal") and began to develop their distinctive twin-guitar style during the now-infamous performances at the Electric Zoo in Wimpton, England. This club is where Tap established their reputation for live performance during the late 1960s. Don't go looking for it, it was torn down in 1969 and turned into a coffee shop. Tap's first live album, *Silent But Deadly*, an acid-rock epic, was recorded here. It was also at the Electric Zoo that David and Nigel's two-hour-dual-solo guitar work on 'Short 'N Easy' was recorded, a solo considered incredibly long ("too long," said one fan) even for 1968.

Nigel and David – the band's twin lead guitarists – developed this unnecessarily ferocious combative guitar style after taking up fencing while on tour. The sound borrows heavily from the lunging attacks and parrying defence used in the sport, a craze which swept across England in the early 1970s. Where Nigel would play higher up the frets, predominantly between numbers 12 and 18, David would remain lower down the neckboard concentrating his performance on frets one through seven. This style of playing unfortunately left frets seven through 12 unplayed, an error that was rectified on the band's next album, *Brainhammer*.

In 1969, after the release of *We Are All Flower People*, the general indifference towards the LP was forgotten following the death of the "great, tall, blond geek with glasses," drummer John "Stumpy" Pepys. Lost to a bizarre gardening accident, "a mystery best left unsolved" according to the authorities, Pepy's death was difficult for the group, but they also saw the funny side to it. "It hits you quite hard to have a member of your group that you've been creatively involved with die. But it's also amusing. Sure. You've got to look at death on the light side once in a while and think: 'Well, sure, he's dead, innit sad? But it's sort of funny, innit.' That's the way I look at it," said Nigel.

Pepys death remains unsolved. The garden responsible is still at large.

- 1 BOTTLE OF BAILEYS (TO BE SHARED WITH CREW)
- 1 PACKET OF WERTHER'S ORIGINALS (FOR THE BAND ONLY)
- AN ASSORTMENT OF YELLOW FLOWERS (ONLY!), ARRANGED IN GREEN VASES (BACKSTAGE ROOM)
- LAVA LAMP (BLUE, YELLOW, GREEN – NO RED!)
- PREVASORE – AS MUCH AS POSSIBLE
- 11 CURLY WURLYS (FOR THE BAND ONLY)

Left: *The band's backstage rider, 1967.*

"WE'VE GOT ARMADILLOS IN OUR TROUSERS. IT'S REALLY QUITE FRIGHTENING."

NIGEL TUFNEL

THE 1970s:
THE RISE OF TAP?

Following the disaster(s) that impacted the success of sophomore album *We Are All Flower People*, and the revolving door(s) of keyboardists and management dismemberment that defined their early period, Spinal Tap entered the 1970s as a new beast, untamed, and ready to play LOUD.

The 1970s was a dreadful decade. For everyone. Vietnam. Hippies. Death of Hippies. Watergate. The Beatles break-up. Floppy disks. VCRs. Pocket calculators. Dead Elvis. Margaret Thatcher. Hosepipe bans. It was just a really shitty time to be alive. And then along came Spinal Tap.

Spinal Tap's core trio – Smalls, Tufnel, St Hubbins – became a dominant gust of wind to be reckoned with in the 1970s releasing an album every single year throughout the decade. Critics may say what they want

about England's loudest band, (and they did, regularly) but you "cannot fault their prolificness, no matter how much you want to," wrote one journalist in 1979. Ten albums in ten years is not a not trivial matter to be scoffed at, even though the albums themselves were scoffed at independently.

Starting with *Brainhammer* in 1970 and climaxing, rather messily, with *Shark Sandwich* in 1980, the decade saw Spinal Tap reach their highest peak (*Intravenus de Milo* goes gold, in sales) but also saw them plunged to

"The '70s were shitty to everyone, right?"

David St Hubbins

their lowest low (*Intravenus de Milo* goes platinum, in returns). With each successful album of diminishing returns, the band always aimed high to make sure they reached the lowest common denominator, usually white American teenage boys.

During the middle of the decade, manager Glyn Hampton-Cross and keyboardist Ross MacLochness left the group to "pursue other, better, interests." "They were fired," noted Nigel bluntly. One member they couldn't fire was drummer Eric "Stumpy Joe" Childs, he left of his own accord after choking to death on someone else's vomit. But for every player who left the group, or died, a new member came along. Viv Savage, Ian Faith, Peter "James" Bond, Mick Shrimpton and tambourinist Jeanine Pettibone all joined the band. And left it. While members came and went during this decade, the one thing that remained consistent was the general lukewarm dissastification of the group's output by critics and fans alike.

While Spinal Tap albums never set the charts alight, in a qualitive or quantative way, their constant touring of North America and Europe, their bread and butter, always put food on the table for the band and cold sore cream on their lips. No one went hungry. Not even salaried players Viv Savage and Mick Shrimpton, who only had a half-vote in band decisions, and had to survive financially on merchandise sales only. Though this ended up being worth more than song royalties come the mid-1970s.

Despite the decade doing a number two on Tap's dream to have a No.1, it was their drunk and horny male fans at their gigs who, as always, were happy to see the cheapest band on the tour circuit, and cheer at the songs they knew. Even if their record label, Megaphone, had stopped answering the band's calls, the fans were (sometimes) always there for them.

It was Megaphone who, in 1968, made the blossoming Spinal Tap's dream come true. They offered

the band a three-figure recording contract (negotiated down from four) and offered the group all the facilities that any struggling record labels can offer: a paltry advance to record an album, a press officer to sweep an scandals under the rug and van-based transportation travel from show to show.

Sadly, this dream was not to last and the Megaphone dream turned to soured cream before becoming a full-on night terror, with the end of the decade collapsing into a heap of acrimony, litigation a lot of name-calling between the two.

There were long-lasting successes though. In 1977, David met the love of his life, and future Tap tambourine player and manager, Jeanine Pettibone. Although, that also ended in acrimony, litigation an lot of name-calling too.

Opposite: *"I'm a real fish nut. I really like fish," says Nigel.*

"I've had my moments in the sky"

Derek Smalls

BRAINHAMMER (1970)

A new decade, a new album, a new Spinal Tap. Moving away from the harmonious acoustic folk-pop and proto-acid-prog rock of the concept album, *We Are All Flower People*, and live album, *Silent But Deadly*, Tap's return to the studio hit the decade with all the shock and awe of a hammer to the brain.

With the songwriting trio of Tufnel, St Hubbins and Smalls now in place, it wasn't long before Tap's musical craftsmenship coagulated into something new. With the 1970s came a new sound, a new form of musical expression, a new way to make tons of money. Heavy metal, as it had been coined had arrived, and Tap were keen to exploit the simplicity of the genre, as well as the trend for a new type of stage costume: Spandex.

Brainhammer's recording process was long and tiring remembers Glyn Hampton-Cross, the band's long-time producer and former friend. "I stuck with the band for as long as I thought they might make some money," he recalled in 1977. "But it was around the recording of *Brainhammer* that I remember thinking that Spinal Tap were simply polishing turds."

It was Hampton-Cross that pushed Spinal Tap into a more metal sound, believing that by replicating the trend for loud guitars, screaming vocals and earache inducing drums would disguise Tap's lack of innovation, while also making money from the rich, white teenage males who, in America at least, were all the rage and most likely to have the disposable inheritance to lap up this new genre. Hampton-Cross wasn't wrong – heavy metal was a money-spinner for several bands in the 1970s. And, for Tap too. Their prolific run of ten albums in ten years made them the biggest band of the decade, in relation to volume of songs recorded, rather than album sales. Hampton-Cross was pivotal at this stage of the band's career, a fact not lost (although mis-remembered) by David: "Glyn was a very interesting bloke. He used to work as an office boy, or a sort of runner, at Megaphone, where we released our first releases. We got to know him. There was a time when it looked he was going to be the head of Megaphone itself, but it didn't work out. He wound up just being head of A&R and he did most of our production as the Thamesmen all the way through Spinal Tap. We then parted ways, mostly because he was more interested in a different kind of sound. But he was a nice bloke."

Featuring the semi-hit singles, 'Big Bottom,' 'Swallow My Love' and 'Lie Back and Take It,' *Brainhammer* didn't do much to improve Spinal Tap's reputation as songwriters, however it greatly improved the band's reputation as "England's Loudest Band," a title they were keen to live up too spectacularly after the release of 1969's *Silent But Deadly*. So when they asked Marshall amplifiers to produce a signature series of amps exclusively for the band, Marshall dutifully accepted. Nigel's request to have the numbers on all the band's amps go one louder – all the way to eleven – was agreed to, despite the bemusement of many of Marshall's technicians. "We thought ten was loud enough," said one. This one-notch louder became the band's trademark volume. Whereas other electric guitarists during this time became revered for creating new and exciting tones from their guitars, it was Nigel who brought the volume. Sadly, Nigel now suffers from severe tinnitus in both ears – and eyes – which is apparent when you speak to him in conversation. "Nigel's not exactly university material, as you know," recalled David. "But people mistake his slow mind for a lack of intelligence, but that's not fair. His lack of intelligence is predominantly down to the sheer volume of white noise that pans between his ears and eyes."

TRACKLIST

1. 'Big Bottom'
2. 'Lie Back and Take It'
3. 'Swallow My Love'
4. 'Brainhammer'
5. 'Lovepunch'
6. 'Fuzzbox'
7. 'Beast With No Name'
8. 'The Clock It Ticks In Time'
9. 'Toad In The Hole'

"We'd love to stand around and chat, but we've gotta sit down in the lobby and wait for the limo."

Terry Ladd

Brainhammer wasn't a complete loss commercially. 'Big Bottom' created seismic waves on FM radio and become a solid-gold Tap classic, selling almost three thousand units in its first three months.

Despite garnering a large amount of stinging criticism from the burgeoning feminist agenda that was currently sweeping mainstream US media, the band remained unfazed, and consistently rejected any sniff of a claim of sexism (not to be confused with sexy-ism).

The feminists got their way (again), and 'Big Bottom' sagged in the charts, reaching only No.35. A victory for women, but also for Spinal Tap, who were happy simply to have a Top 40 hit under their belts. And we'd all agree that that's where 'Big Bottom' belongs.

"YOU KNOW, SEVERAL DOZENS OF PEOPLE SPONTANEOUSLY COMBUST EACH YEAR. IT'S JUST NOT REALLY WIDELY REPORTED."

DAVID ST HUBBINS

NERVE DAMAGE (1971)

With no hit singles, and no non-hit singles, *Nerve Damage* was released less than 12 months after *Brainhammer*. Bad production, bad mixing, and worst of all, bad songwriting left Tap's fourth album as one for the connoisseurs' collection only. And, regrettably, they won't be able to find it either….

Following a few years' touring the "world and elsewhere," when it came to writing and recording *Brainhammer*'s follow-up the band were even more creatively spent than usual. Long-time producer and occasional friend, Glyn Hampton-Cross, tried to "do an Eno" and introduce his own version of Eno's infamous card game Oblique Strategies with the group. Whereas Eno's concept was simplistic: each card offered musicians challenges to break creative blocks by encouraging lateral thinking, Hampton-Cross's concept was a little more oblique – the rules and strategy of which were never written down, nor remembered by anyone in the band, having totally repressed any memory of it. Smalls remembers

"Megaphone – what a bunch of, um, mega-phoneys."

David St Hubbins

something about, "a deck of cards used to represent fruit, or animals, or something, but with unhealthy amounts of abuse and violence if you got an answer wrong," but the rest remains a mystery. Hampton-Cross called his cruelty-based card game "Obscure Analogies" and for a few days it coaxed Nigel, Derek and David, plus new recruit, drummer Eric "Stumpy Joe" Childs, sufficiently out of their creative slump to write and record the minimum requirement of 12 songs to create an album. The card game also inspired the name of the album, *Nerve Damage*, as it believed that was also one of the side-effects of the game.

While the writing and recording of the album felt a lot like torture, management at the band's record label, Megaphone, were in tandem preparing the torturous news that the album would only receive a "limited distribution" upon release. Though the labels' executives were legally obliged to never discuss what that meant precisely, the Spinal Tap Fan Club members, all six of them, deduced that only 500 copies of the album were ever pressed. Worse news was to follow.

Megaphone refused to print and distribute any

singles from the record, nor release any funds for the marketing of the album. This angered the group, in particular Nigel, whose remark, "What Bastards," inspired St Hubbins to write the song 'What Bastards,' a late inclusion on the album, and a song that name-checks all of Megaphone's executives as, rather bizarrely, "horse-riding, gondola-paddling snot-gobblers" and a lot worse to boot. This, in turn, angered Megaphone personnel, naturally, who instantly abandoned the album upon the release and have since deleted the master recordings. As always, the fight between the "suits" and the "talent" is bad news for the band's fans who simply want to enjoy *Nerve Damage*. As the album is still nowhere to be seen or heard on the black or bootleg market, Tapheads will have to use their own wits to locate the album.

After receiving a press release from executives at Megaphone requesting them to boycott their own release – a first for the music industry – *Nerve Damage* was ignored by critics too, and signalled the beginning of a "three-year musical plummet into the abyss," for Tap, with the general consensus that *Nerve Damage* "suffered from the certain sameness that set in during Tap's meteoric rise to the middle of the pack," wrote Basingstoke's premier music magazine, *Stoked*.

However, 1971 wasn't all doom and gloom for Spinal Tap. A three-date World Tour "around England's home counties" was considered a success. With Tap having been vindicated by Megaphone's vindictive agenda against them, the band entered the year 1972 with a new fire in their belly desperate to prove to Megaphone, and their fans, that Tap still had some gas left in their tanks.

TRACKLIST

1. 'CNS (Central Nervous System)'
2. 'Doom and Gloom'
3. 'Wide Fingers'
4. 'Shockaholic'
5. 'A&E (for U&I)'
6. 'Aloha (Hello and Goodbye)'
7. 'Question Time'
8. 'Upside Down (The Wrong Way Round)'
9. 'Fortune Teller Blues'
10. 'Bowels of Hell'
11. 'What Bastards'
12. 'Dutch Courage'

Opposite: *Official band merchandise in the 80s.*

Tap Up Close:
Viv Savage

Viv Savage's 1975–1982 tenure as Tap's seventh keyboardist oversaw the band's second stab at success, following the band's third regroup on the strength of surprise No.12 US hit single 'Nice 'N Stinky.' A US tour to support *Bent for the Rent* followed, and Viv's prodigious keys' playing was the key to unlocking the lock that opened the door for Tap to unlock a new sound. Sadly, Viv's history as a child drummer would haunt him to death when he was an adult, suffering a fate equal to death, by dying in the same vein as Tap's other drummers.

Following Derek Smalls' confusing and conflicted feelings towards religion, Tap returned to the studio in 1977 to record a religious concept album called *Rock 'n' Roll Creation*, or *The Gospel According to Tap*, depending on what international distribution market you live in. Following the dismissal of Ross MacLochness, Viv Savage, the former keyboardist with Aftertaste (Viv left the group after bitter disagreements with the lead singer), and his velvety organ skills – and more than 300 pre-programmed sounds on his Yamaha K3240 keyboard – helped imbue Tap's most recent album with all the "churchy" qualities required to make the record sound sincere and genuine, even if it was obviously a desperate cash in on a new un-Tapped market (religious albums were all the rage then). The band needed a hit album and "Religious people tend to have more money than atheists," was the band's view.

An odd character, but a child musical prodigy, it is believed Viv learnt to play the keyboard before his first birthday, excluding time spent in the womb. After conquering keyboard, Viv turned his attention to other musical instrumentation families, woodwind, then brass, before settling on percussion. For years, Viv tuned his ears to the sounds of beating drums, a decision that ultimately cost him his life. It was only when he was aged 15 that Viv returned to his first instrument, the keys, after developing severe, and unsightly, bicep issues following years of playing drums as a baby. While he yearned to play music, the by-products of rock 'n' roll became too much.

As, with all great musical talents comes addictive personalities and, alas, Viv's love of his own addictions were addictive. "Viv is the great procurer

"Have a good time all the time. That's my philosophy, Marty!"

Viv Savage

Left: *Viv, pictured here enjoying 'Mendocino Rocket Fuel.'*

of certain road necessities," Derek admitted on camera to DiBergi's film crew, much to Viv's wife's dismay. His addiction to "Mendocino rocket fuel" and "Gold Rush Brown" while never spiralling out of control, did amplify Viv's already clown-esque and zany personality defects. Viv himself admitted that he can be a bit OTT at times. "I'd probably get a bit stupid and start to make a fool of myself in public if there wasn't a stage to go on," admitted Viv, during *This Is Spinal Tap*, much to his wife's dismay (again), when asked what would he do without rock 'n' roll in his life.

Upon Nigel's brief departure from the group in 1982, during the cursed *Smell the Glove* North American Tour, it was Viv who stepped up to the plate, and licked it clean, when asked to fill in on Nigel's bass-playing part for 'Big Bottom' (it was a dual-bass song). "Oh, yeah. I've got two hands here, yeah, I can do it," Viv said with a firm grasp of his own hands and saving the band from the embarrassment of playing 'Big Bottom' with only one bassline part. This is how Derek, Nigel and David would love to remember Viv – as a consummate professional – but sadly, the curse of Tap drummers is a cruel master and you can't run or hide from her (it's a female curse).

In 1992, Viv died in a natural gas explosion while visiting the grave of Tap drummer Mick Shrimpton (1977–82). "The curse, somehow, if there is a curse, knew that Viv was hiding the fact that he played drums," said Derek in later interview. "If we'd known that, we never would have hired him."

Viv's tombstone is inscribed with his motto, "Have a good time, all the time," a fitting tribute to a man whose freakish death left a huge hole in Spinal Tap's heart. However, after learning what an administrative headache, and cost, it would be to hire a new keyboardist the band decided that Viv's seat would remain unfilled for more than a decade. "How can we replace, Viv?" Nigel said poignantly after his death. "No, seriously, we literally can't afford to replace him."

"Quite exciting, this computer magic!"

Viv Savage

Left: *The band share more than just thrilling moments on stage.*

BLOOD TO LET (1972)

Locked into a position of an increasingly stale stalemate with Megaphone in 1971, Spinal Tap were left twiddling their thumbs in 1972. The band members had each other, sure, but that only made things worse…

Watergate. Hurricane Agnes. Bloody Friday. And Sunday. Cod Wars. The year 1972 was a pretty dreadful year for everyone who was alive. But for Derek, David, Nigel, and Eric "Stumpy Joe" Childs, life remained fairly static. They had been on the road touring England's home counties (for three shows) in 1971 and delighting their countryside fans with *Nerve Damage*, oblivious to the changing world that surrounded them.

Despite frosty relations with record label Megaphone, the band were allowed to record a new album, as long as, according to the band's then-manager Freddie Steak, "they tried really hard to write songs that would not lose the record label any more money." Steak continued: "They knew if they failed with *Blood To Let*, they would be dropped from the label, and unlikely to be picked up by anyone else, considering Megaphone were already the most unsuccessful label in the industry."

Wanting another shot at international success, as well the money to go on a tour outside of the UK's home counties, Spinal Tap did the one thing most bands do when they're in a bind. They decamped to Los Angeles to record an album, undistracted from all the noise of ex-wives, ex-girlfriends, ex-loan sharks, record label executives and first cousins who may, or may not, allegedly be suing a member of the band for child support.

With the fresh Los Angeles air filling their lungs, and golden sunshine de-whitening their pale British frames, the members of Spinal Tap were able to record their new LP infused with new sights, sounds and smells of the US of A.

For the three-week process, recording the songs took between twelve and sixteen hours a day, depending on the length of Nigel's guitar solos: each solo had to be completed in one long take, rather than edited and spliced together as was then common practise in the recording industry. "It makes the solo more authentic," Nigel said in the studio. "If the solo is played in its

Above: *Tap get snapped.*

Opposite: *Fisting: Smalls, Tufnel and St Hubbins.*

entirety in one take, the listener may not hear the difference, and Glyn, our producer, may get very irate with me, but I'm a professional musician, and my guitar solos are my babies. You wouldn't cut up and splice babies together would you? No, you make them in one take. It's exactly the same with guitar solos."

With no gigs booked while recording the album, the members of Tap would travel across Los Angeles to various "Open Mic Nights" to perform their newest songs. 'Low Blow,' 'Blood to Let' and 'Bunslinger' were all tested in front of unsuspecting audiences at some of LA's smallest bars and most unhygienic live music clubs, such as The Dankpit and The Wiper Room. The band, playing under various aliases such as Alias and Mr StageName, while wearing wigs, beards and typical LA fashions – Derek grew his famous Fu Manchu moustache during this period, a popular fixture of the LA facial hair scene – so they could go unnoticed among their LA fans, many of whom didn't show up, because they had no way of knowing they were playing, due to their unnecessary deployment of band aliases.

Sadly, despite experiencing the sights, sounds and smells of the edgy LA club atmosphere, the band failed to absorb any of it and cranked out an album that the LAAP (Los Angeles Associated Press) described as, "a mundane collection of songs that sounds like a Spinal Tap tribute band who aren't very good at their jobs." Thankfully, *Blood to Let* outperformed the band's three previous albums, selling almost 700 copies in one day, giving Megaphone the confidence to retain Tap's services for another album…a decision they would absolutely come to regret.

TRACKLIST

1. **'Blood to Let'**
2. **'I for an I'**
3. **'Bunslinger'**
4. **'Low Blow"**
5. **"Tightfit"**
6. **'Fire In The Hole'**
7. **'Bloodshot Between the Eyes'**
8. **'Bells Go Ring'**
9. **'Out For Blood'**
10. **'She Means It'**

Those That Were There: Polymer Records

Bobbi Flekman, Polymer Records' "hostess with the mostest" and A&R officer, first met Spinal Tap at a welcome reception in their honour in New York, to celebrate the completion of *Smell the Glove*. A living, breathing (though, as a chain smoker, not for long) embodiment of the yuppie culture that was all the rage in North America in the 1980s, Bobbi, alongside PR agent Artie Fufkin, were assigned to the band to make ensure their comeback album for Polymer did better business (i.e. any) than 1980's poorly received *Shark Sandwich*.

The 1980s was a good time to be in a glam metal band, or what the critics called "poodle rock." The genre had risen to chart dominance with acts such as Death Matrix, Van Bang, Poison Lace, Reprobates, Monsterlove and Sweatshop. While it was true, that the market was oversaturated with this new genre of music, for Polymer Records, signing Spinal Tap was a no-brainer: Surely a band that had been so unsuccessful for so long, but remained together, were due a comeback of some kind. It wasn't going to be an easy ride, but with Bobbi Flekman now onboard to guide the band back to the charts, or at least to a money-spinning tour, their first in the US in six years, the group now had a fighting chance of gaining new teenage, white male fans, fans who were lapping glam metal as fast as their tongues could lap.

Bobbi's first task as Tap's A&R guru was to inform the band's manager, Ian Faith, that Polymer were "rather down" on *Smell the Glove's* cover, and that it wasn't going to fly with major US retail outlets, as well as everyone else. "They find it very offensive and very sexist," Bobbi informed Ian, much to his surprise. "I don't care what the band wanted to do," Bobbi told Ian, rather bluntly, but then it was the 1980s when straight talking was all the rage. Or as Bobbi would say, repeatedly, "Money talks and bullshit walks."

As a woman herself, and a feminist, Bobbi had a personal bitterness towards *Smell the Glove*, a fact she made visibly clear to Ian Faith. "I don't think that a sexy cover is the answer for why an album sells or doesn't sell because you tell me...the *White Album*, what was that? There was nothing on that goddamn cover." Despite Ian's protestations that "every cut on the album

is a hit," it was Bobbi's over-dramatic, irrational female perspective of the album cover that gave Denis Eton-Hogg concerns of the media backlash should the album be released as the band desired. It was Bobbi who asked Polymer's designers to "experiment with the packaging" of the album. She told Ian: "You know, we can probably work something out. I'll talk to Dennis and maybe we can come up with a compromise. A new design concept that we can all live with." The new design concept, as we know now, was drastically altered from a greased-up woman sniffing a black glove to a plain black square that resembled "something you wear around your arm, you don't put this on your fucking turntable," admonished David. Ian remained upbeat about the situation: "I frankly think that this is the turning point, okay? We're on our way now. It's time to kick arse!" Nigel could see past the colour of the album's skin, however, and judged the cover solely on its blackness. "There is something about this, that's that's so black, it's like; 'How much more black could this be?' And the answer is none, none more black."

When Spinal Tap reappeared in 1992 to promote their new album *Break Like the Wind*, distributed by their own independent record label, Dead Faith, Nigel had heard on the grapevine that Bobbi's career had hit the skids after working with Tap, tarnished by the association, and she was unable to get another job in the industry. She was now working as a mortician's receptionist in New Jersey. "If she hadn't been a cheat, a liar and a bitch, she would have been a great girl," said Nigel conclusively.

Far right: *Sir Denis Eaton-Hogg, founder of Hoggwood.*

"Money talks and bullshit walks."

Bobbi Flekman

"SO, WHEN YOU'RE PLAYING YOU FEEL LIKE A PRESERVED MOOSE ON STAGE?"

MARTY DIBERGI

Above: Intravenus de Milo – *a cover that, ironically, many critics were up in arms about.*

Released two years after *Blood to Let*, *Intravenus de Milo* was not the critical comeback the band had hoped for. The album received the ire of many music critics, with one major music publication slinging several word-turds at Tap's musical baby, criticizing the band inside and out: "The album's tasteless cover is a good indication of the lack of musical invention within. The musical growth of this band cannot be charted. They are treading water in a sea of retarded sexuality and bad poetry."

As captured in Marty DiBergi's "rockumenatry" about the band, Nigel's response to this review was

blind fans could see the guitarist was visibly hurt by the criticism, despite years of becoming ignorant to criticism.

Despite the sharp slings and arrows of the music press, *Intravenus de Milo* became the first album to go gold (two levels below platinum), no doubt in part thanks to the album's unforgettable – and to many, unforgivable – cover: the *Venus de Milo* sculpture with an IV tube connected to her stump. Unlike the *Venus de Milo* herself, many art fans were up in arms about the desecration and depiction of Alexandros of Antioch's beloved statue, claiming the cover was "a publicity stunt to sell mediocre music," the type of art stunt that modern contemporary artists would be ashamed to pull. As it happens, the group were confused as to why the album cover, designed by avant-garde design studio OnGarde!, caused such outrageous offense.

Following the album's (relative) success in July, led by the lead single and classic rock paean to underage objects of affection, 'Tonight I'm Gonna Rock You's' infectious chorus, verses, and guitar solos, Tap's then-manager Freddie Steak rushed to book and promote a European tour to satisfy the Tap supply and demand that suddenly had emerged. "Tap were back!" Derek remarked to a journalist. "I'm not surprised, though. Everything in life is circular, revolutionary. Anything that stays at the back of the shelf for a long time always comes back to the front, when all the good stuff is gone. It's basic economics."

A hurried tour, and hiring of keyboardist Ross MachLochness (ex-Kilt Kids), followed in the

TRACKLIST

1. 'Tonight I'm Gonna Rock You Tonight'
2. 'Saliva of the Fittest'
3. 'Karma Sutra'
4. 'A Tragedy in B Minor'
5. 'Treasure Chest'
6. 'Greased Up With Nowhere To Go'
7. 'Gift Horse'
8. 'Spread Eagle'
9. 'Heavin' and Ho'ing'
10. 'Tap Attack!'
11. 'Bootlicker'
12. 'Knockin' On Death's Door'

London Music Membrane
11 December 1966
7.30 til late (9pm)
All seats reserved
£2

PUDDING
PEPYS
UPHAM
TUFNEL
ST HUBBINS
=
SPINAL TAP
Their first ever gig!
SEE THEM NOW BEFORE THEY HIT THE BIG TIME AND DISAPPEAR FOREVER!

TICKETS ON SALE NOW!

were booked into 10,000, 15,000-seat venues, which of course never sold out. "When the album did well, our manager Freddie didn't," David claimed at the time. "He wasn't used to managing a successful band, so he had no experience of what to do and how to manage us as the proper rock stars we had become. We had to let him go, which was tough, because he had been with us since the beginning. But it was also easy, because we were famous and didn't care about hurting his feelings."

With Freddie Steak out and the band captain-less at the height of their fame, it wasn't long before the band hit an iceberg of the non-lettuce variety. The album, with sales of one-and-a-half million, had also incurred one million copies returned to stores, the first album in history to go gold in sales, but platinum in returns. Unfazed by this "obvious administrative error," the band still had a platinum album on their hands, and no one was going to tell them otherwise. However, the returns debacle made it apparent that a new buffer between band and everyone else was needed. The group knew they needed a new kick-ass manager, somebody who could acquiesce to their every request, but also keep the "plebs" away from them and their "negative vibes."

This urgent responsibility landed in the reliable hands of Ian Faith, the former manager of 12-year-old metallers from Northampton, Dirtbone, who Ian had led victorious at Battle of the Bands at Kettering Town Hall that year.

With their new manager-butler in place, Tap completed their North American and European tour,

and saw out 1974 in spectacular fashion, performing a New Year's Eve show at The Bucket on Squatney Road, in Squatney, the venue of David and Nigel's first-ever gig together, a decade before. The gig was deemed a success because the band's mums and dads showed up, even the divorced ones with new partners. With a bona fide hit in 'Tonight I'm Gonna Rock You Tonight' sitting pretty at the middle of the lower end of the US *Billboard* chart, Spinal Tap were riding high into 1975 – they were unstoppable. But then disaster struck...

Drummer Eric "Stumpy Joe" Childs was found dead. The official explanation was that he choked to death on vomit. Not his own, but somebody else's. At the end of the funeral, Stumpy Joe's body was buried in a coffin full of vomit. "Stumpy died in his own vomit, we felt he should be buried in his own vomit. It's what he would have wanted," Derek said. As the coffin was lowered into the ground, Nigel, David and Derek performed a 21-drum salute in honour of their fallen comrade. They invoiced Eric's wife directly for this act at the end of the month. "We don't do gigs for free," Derek wrote in attached letter, "but we did charge you mate's rates. It's what Stumpy Joe would have wanted."

TAPHEADS

Whatever critics and regular people on the street may think of Spinal Tap's music, the only opinion that matters to the band is that of their fans, a motley crew of predominantly young white boys, and older educated professionals, who call themselves Tapheads.

While Spinal Tap's popularity has waned, dipped, dived, and hit rock bottom over the decades, there have been a group of boys (now men, but also still a lot of boys) who have remained loyal to the band since their first album back in 1967. As pondered in Marty DiBergi's "rockumentary," *This Is Spinal Tap*, the group believe their fan base respect them, not because they love their music, but because the respect the members as alpha males – men with big ol' swingin' dicks. "Really they're quite fearful – that's my theory," mused Nigel. "Our fans see us on stage with tight trousers we've got, you know, armadillos in our trousers, I mean

it's really quite frightening..." But it's not just young boys who adore the band, there is a long list (albeit on a small bit of paper) of celebrity fans who routinely turn up at the band's shows, looking for drugs. "Benny Hill was a fan a long time ago," David has said, without verifying his source. "Dennis Hopper often travelled with us. Frankie Howerd, Nicolas Cage, Lenny Kravitz and Walter Matthau – they all can't keep away from our gigs, or have been Tap fans in the past. I know that for

Below: *Music fans watching a band play music.*

Opposite: *Backstage rider, circa 2003.*

50ML DOSES OF THE FOLLOWING:

- DOXAZOSIN
- MEPERIDINE
- DRONEDARONE
- CLOMIPRAMINE
- CHLORPHENIRAMINE
- TRIHEXYPHENIDYL
- CHLORPROMAZINE
- PENTOBARBITAL
- ESZOPICLONE

- DIGOXIN
- DIPYRIDAMOLE
- CHLORDIAZEPOXIDE
- ERGOT MESYLATE
- FAMOTIDINE
- METHYLTESTOSTERONE
- 4 BAGS OF MARSHMALLOWS (PINK ONES ONLY)

Below: *A Taphead sticks their fingers up at the band.*

a fact. Someone told me that and I believe them."

If you look out among the crowd during one of the band's most recent (1992) *Break Like the Wind* tours, you'll see a much wider demographic of fans than had ever bothered to show up before. Tap's new-found maturity has brought with it a new wave of mature fans, all eager to sweat out their mature frustrations (work, failed marriages, children, money worries, etc.) while throwing off the shackles of the daily grind, and throwing punches at strangers in the moshpit. Nigel has said: "Our music appeals to professionals – a neuro-surgeon, a stockbroker, businessmen who are serious about life. Serious people. The Illuminati…and, yes, the occasional 14-year-old white boy."

Even if age, socio-economic factors, race and gender divide the band's fans in the real world, what unites them all at a Tap gig is their shared love for England's loudest band. They are Tapheads one and all. Outside the band's Philadelphia show in 1982, Marty DiBergi captured a fan's love for their favourite band on film. "It's like you become one with the guys in the band," the fan, an uneducated blonde woman, and clearly high, said: "I mean there's no division, the music just unites people with the players."

With Tapheads sticking by the band's side no matter how many unpopular albums they release, no matter how many members leave, no matter how many gigs are cancelled, one thing is sure: Spinal Tap have the easiest-to-please fans in the world.

"In 1966, I went down to Greenwich Village, New York City, to a rock club called the Electric Banana … I heard a band that for me redefined the word 'rock 'n' roll.'"

Marty DiBergi, former Taphead

"THERE'S SOMETHING ABOUT THIS THAT'S SO BLACK, IT'S LIKE 'HOW MUCH MORE BLACK COULD THIS BE?' AND THE ANSWER IS NONE. NONE MORE BLACK."

NIGEL TUFNEL

THE SUN NEVER SWEATS (1975)

Following hot on the heels of 1974's *Intravenus de Milo*, *The Sun Never Sweats* saw Tap step comfortably into the shoes as 'the voice of a generation.' Sadly, the album's shocking production – deafening drums but eerily quiet vocals – meant that none of their fans could hear what that voice was saying. A time of personnel upheaval, Glyn Hampton-Cross's tenure as producer came to an end. Drummer Peter "James" Bond also left the band. He died.

Recorded at the end of a successful North American and European tour, with their big balls swinging high and sweaty in the air, *The Sun Never Sweats* was the victory lap at the end of a triumphant two years for Tap. While their first concept album, *We Are All Flower People*, was a hot mess and a critical and commercial flop, …*Sweats* is a broader concept.

Centred around themes of 'Rule Britannia,' the album features the pomp rock magic of previous Tap hits, 'Tonight I'm Gonna Rock You' and 'Big Bottom,' but instead of lustful sex and dirty rock 'n' roll imagery at the fore, this time the British Empire takes centre stage. Gone are the lengthy and extravagant guitar solos and bass breaks, replaced now by musical quotations from 'The British Grenadiers' and spliced sounds of trumpets, horns and gun salutes, found when

Derek and Nigel went looking through the BBC's royalty-free sound archives.

The album's cover stands erect as one of the band's most respectful, and least insulting. Gone were the OTT visuals of *Brainhammer* (a man literally hammering a brain). Now the band walk along a massive Union Jack towards the setting sun. The lead single, 'Stonehenge' explored the themes of ancient Druid traditions and practices, while second single 'Daze of Knights of Old' elucidates on themes of King Arthur's era and why his table was round, and not rectangular, like most tables.

The record's title came from a mishearing by Derek, someone who has read widely and deeply on England's history, and was the chief songwriter of this album following Nigel and David's repetitive strain

injuries incurred during the power-chord heavy songs of *Intravenus de Milo* and *Blood to Let*. Derek recalled about the title: "When we were backstage at one of shows during our 'Home Counties' tour in '72. I said 'The sun never sets on the British empire,' but the rest of the guys thought I said 'sweats.' Now, every time I say the word 'set' they change it to 'sweats.' It's a nightmare when we're trying to discuss the setlist, as you can imagine. It's a little tour prank the band does. Frankly, I find it fucking upsweating. See, now even I'm doing it."

With Tap's fans growing (in numbers) both at home and abroad, in September '75, the band embarked on a Far East jaunt to try and karate-chop the Asian market in two. The resulting tour was captured on the live triple album, *Jap Habit*, the band's most racially insensitive album title to chart. Recorded during the band's two-week tour of Japan, the Philippines, Hong Kong, Malaysia and a one-off gig somewhere unpronounceable in China, the album stayed on the 112 slot of the US *Billboard* chart for 82 of its 84 weeks. "You can't buy that kind of consistency," Nigel said of the album's chart consistency. *Jap Habit* includes the single "Nice 'N Stinky," which in 1977 became a surprise hit in the United States, following its strange inclusion on the band's religious album, *Rock 'n' Roll Creation*. The innuendo-laden track stands out amongst the other gospel-based songs. For the British release of *Jap Habit*, 2lbs of packaging, such as a paper kimono and pieces of raw fish, were included with each purchased album, which caused a notable stink with retailers and distributors. The packaging was vetoed by Megaphone for the American release, and the album was cut back to

a double album to try and scrape back profits lost on the UK release. Following the success of *Jap Habit* and the Far East tour, the debacle surrounding the unlistenable production mix of *The Sun Never Sweats* further divided the band from manager Glyn Hampton-Cross. "We did part ways after *Sweats*," David recalled. "Glyn was more interested in a different sound. What he wanted to do was build our audience, make it broader, he wanted us to start singing Broadway tunes. We all thought it was a bum idea, frankly. We were no longer on the same page, or even book. Or one of those things that's bigger than a book. A tome? We were no longer on the same tome. So we fired him."

Hampton-Cross was out. The band would self-produce their next few albums, much to Megaphone's dismay. The year 1975 also saw the departure of keyboardist Ross MacLochness to pursue other interests, which included becoming a missionary in Namibia. "We haven't heard from him since," David admitted. "Well, we get a postcard every few months, but we haven't *heard* from him since.

TRACKLIST

1. 'Daze of Knights of Old'
2. 'The Princess and the Unicorn'
3. 'Bow Bells'
4. 'The Sun Never Sweats'
5. 'Stonehenge'
6. 'Maiden England'
7. 'So Sorry Mrs Dorry'
8. 'Back to School'
9. 'The Pearly King'
10. 'Ring Roads and Roundabouts'

Opposite: *Faces only a mother could love.*

"Making a big thing out of it would have been a good idea."

Derek Smalls

"Fuck the napkin!"

Ian Faith

"Nigel gave me a drawing that said 18 inches. Now, whether or not he knows the difference between feet and inches is not my problem. I do what I'm told!"

Ian Faith

Tap Up Close:
Mick Shrimpton

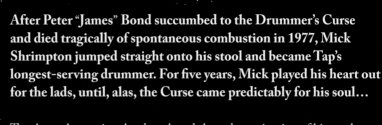

After Peter "James" Bond succumbed to the Drummer's Curse and died tragically of spontaneous combustion in 1977, Mick Shrimpton jumped straight onto his stool and became Tap's longest-serving drummer. For five years, Mick played his heart out for the lads, until, alas, the Curse came predictably for his soul…

Thanks to the passion, hard work and sheer determination of his mother and father nine months previously, Mick Shrimpton was born in December 1948. Years later, that sweet little baby would turn into a deeply-perverted substance abuser whose love of narcotics would cause concern for the band throughout his tenure sitting on his stool. However, the band were more upset with Mick's chronic lateness rather than his debilitating drug addiction. "He is a drummer, he should turn up early, if anything," Nigel exclaimed. "No, I mean, on time. He should arrive only on time."

Erratic timekeeping and severe addiction to drugs aside, Mick was the perfect drummer. Mick's solid playing came from his years of experience as the former house drummer for the Eurovision Song Contest. It was during the filming of DiBergi's "rockumentary" that the real Mick was allowed to shine, giving the viewers a deep insight into Mick's life with Tap. Interviewed in the bathtub, DiBergi asked Mick if he "feared for his life," in relation to the the Curse of Tap drummers. Mick, ever the professional, replied: "When I did join, you know, they did tell me, they kind of took me aside and said 'Well, Mick, ah, you know it's like this' and it did kind of freak me out a bit, but it can't always happen to everyone, can it? The law of averages says that you will survive."

Unfortunately, Mick's misunderstanding of mathematical probability got the better of him, and during the band's ill-fated Japanese leg of their ill-fated 1982 North American 14-date tour, Mick Shrimpton was struck by the Curse and died in a mysterious on-stage explosion which left only his stool behind...a stool that would later be sat on by Mick's brother, Ric.

His death was caught on camera by DiBergi's film crew. Many fans, at first, thought that DiBergi had used primitive CGI effects to fake Mick's death to end the film with a real bang. However, Mick's death via explosion was real. He was dead.

Mick Shrimpton, a drummer who lived too fast, and drummed too slow, a chronically unpunctual man whose drug abuse sped up his death, died the way he didn't live – on time.

"As long as there's sex and drugs, I can do without the rock and roll."

Mick Shrimpton

BENT FOR THE RENT (1976)

What goes up, must come down. After the awesome (and legal) highs of *Intravenus de Milo*, *Jap Habit* and *The Sun Never Sweats*, Spinal Tap were faced once again with the sour lows of the poor-selling, glam record *Bent for the Rent*. The band were now leaving skid marks on the bottom of their topsy-turvy rollercoaster career; they had finally reached their inevitable nadir, a low that would last until 1992.

1976 was a bumper* year for Spinal Tap. Though they remained prolific songwriters, releasing two albums in 12 months, the quality of both albums suffered, no doubt at the hands of their prolificness. After the 'British Empire'-based concept album of *The Sun Never Sweats* was a hit with fans old and new, Tap were reinvigorated and re-energized: they had the Midas touch, whatever they touched turned to gold sales. This over-confidence, swelled by a massive intake of legal highs, gave the band an idea. Looking for a new sound – but not Broadway tunes, as Glyn Hampton-Cross had suggested – they were to ditch their usual twin-guitar heavy metal sound and swap it for "glitter-rock" or "glam," the latest fad that was sweeping American and European nations, and exemplified by the popular movie, *Glam Grandmas (*known as *GlamMa*s in the UK), about a group of senior citizens who turn their nursing home into a successful nightclub. The movie's soundtrack was a hit, and a new musical craze was born.

Turning their backs on their rock 'n' roll roots, and wanting to exploit this new musical craze for "dire financial needs," Tap searched for a new keyboardist, "someone who could add synthesized sounds to smother Nigel and David's loud guitars" said Derek.

Viv Savage, formerly of Aftertaste, got the sweet job, and he became a close friend to the band, not least for his abilities as a "great procurer of certain road necessities," Derek's less-than-subtle reference to "Mendocino Rocket Fuel" and Viv's less-than-subtle name for cocaine.

Hosting a bevy of disco-heavy, but melody-sparse songs, such as 'When a Man Looks Like a Woman,'

* The author means bumpy.

TRACKLIST

1. 'When a Man Looks Like a Woman'
2. 'High Heels, Hot Wheels'
3. 'Heavy Duty'
4. 'Bent for the Rent'
5. 'The Lord Taketh'
6. 'Blown To Bits'
7. 'I Don't Regret Much, (But I Do Regret That)'
8. 'One Eye Open'
9. 'Dinosore'
10. 'Wet Patch'

Opposite: *Nigel's laser eye surgery had strange side effects.*

Above: *David's* Namesake Series *cassettes.*

'High Heels, Hot Wheels' and, of course, the hard-hitting glam metal monster with a groove, 'Heavy Duty,' *Bent for the Rent* was, in David's words, "part of the last dribble of the glam age."

With Tap's eighth album sliding down the back of pan to greet the group's other albums, the band were desperate for funds to support their next tour. New manager, Ian Faith, in an OTT show of aggression to display loyalty to the band, went all out: he decided to sue Megaphone for back royalties owed since the gold status of *Intravenus de Milo*. With no evidence to back up this claim, the bold move backfired. Instead, Megaphone countersued the band for "lack of talent." Plenty of evidence is available to support this claim, and Tap and Faith are swiftly taken to court, resulting in

Tap having to perform under the name the Cadburys until the settlement with Megaphone was reached. The case was eventually forgotten about in the summer of 1977 due to everyone being in America too wrapped up in the success of new sci-fi fantasy epic, *War Stars*, the story of white, blond, American teenager (Tap's main audience) who goes on a quest across the universe to defeat an evil overlord, who turns out to be his first cousin. But the damage had been done. The band's faith in Faith was shaken and their relationship remained strained for the next few years, a truth made crystal in DiBergi's *This Is Spinal Tap* "rockumentary."

Other distractions also led to the poor-songwriting of *Bent*. At the beginning of the recording process, director Marco Zamboni cast Derek in his motion picture, *Roma 79*. The film features Derek, dressed completely in white robes, portraying an assassin who is gunned down before the opening credits. It's a non-speaking role, except for Derek's death screams. It was David and Nigel's critique of Derek's performance in this film, or to be more accurate, Derek's "lack of thrust in his power zone," which prompted Derek to insert a zucchini down his trousers to amplify his visible dick lines (VDL), as captured in Marty DiBergi's 1982 "rockumentary." Derek pleaded with DiBergi to delete this scene, but the director was untrained in his film editing software at the time and didn't know how.

With *Bent for the Rent* stinking up the US, UK, AU, EU, SA and USSR charts, Spinal Tap did the one thing no one was expecting, nor wanting, them to do. They released another album.

TAP DANCING (1976)

Just when Spinal Tap thought that 1976 couldn't get any worse, they released *Tap Dancing*, the group's worst received record. The record's failure hit the band where it hurts: right in the nuts.

The inspiration behind Tap Dancing – *a glitterball.*

"It's not available anymore, and it never will be," David said the day after the release of *Tap Dancing*. "It's the album we dare not speak of, like the 'Scottish play' by Shakespeare; we never say the album's name out loud. We've had enough bad luck – just like Macbeth with those witches."

Tapheads found Tap's newly-discovered disco direction a step too far in the wrong direction. "It had Bargain Bin written all over it," Derek said, in an apology to weekly music magazine, *MNE*.

Over-produced by trendy disco producer Felix the Hat (real name Malcolm Clark), *Tap Dancing's* ten songs were loaded with many of the standard bleats, beeps, blips and bops that defined the mid-1970s disco scene, but also had Nigel and David's trademark rock 'n' roll guitar and vocal scowls and screams implanted over the top, simultaneously offering two conflicting types of genres in tandem at once. "It was a mess," admitted David. It was Nigel who suffered the worse abuse from music reviewers, however. They took to the airwaves and print media to vent their spleen over the musician's first attempt at writing a "Mach" piece (a fusion of Mozart and Bach) on the track, "Too Wet To Get Hard." The critics were united in hatred: "The song is decent attempt at classical orchestration for piano, with a gliding melody at its heart, but it is ruined by the producer's pounding rhythms and piercing whistles inextricably juxtaposed on top of it all. It seems neither the song's author, or album's producer, knew what they wanted or how to achieve it, and showing no constraint in getting there either."

The album appeared at No.199 in the US *Billboard* chart, but slipped the next day into the Top 500, and then disappeared entirely from everywhere the day after. "Rock 'n' roll is not an exact science," Ian Faith recalled in an interview during the time, defending the album. "It's not a science at all, in fact. If the band had a magic formula for success, don't you think they'd have used it by now? For every album? I keep them telling to write good songs, but they don't. Not because they can't or won't, or because they don't want to, but because it's not up to them. It's up to the God of Rock 'n' roll, or the Devil, a higher power, you know?"

Following a dismal performance on the UK's early morning children's music show *PopDisease!*, which resulted in the band throwing punches at each other during the pre-recording of 'Glamtasm' – a song about a spectre possessed by the soul of disco – Spinal Tap cancelled their ten-date European tour. This didn't go down well with the tour's sponsor, Ibruflex, a pain-

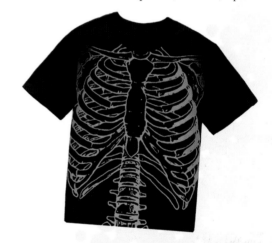

"This is my exact inner structure, done in a t-shirt. Exactly medically accurate. See?"

Nigel Tufnel

relieving headache tablet brand. The irony was lost on the band, but not with the multinational pharmaceutical parent company who took Tap to court, causing even more headaches for the band. Thankfully, the group

had had already received their free promotional samples from Ibruflex, and could at least self-medicate.

With their reputation in tatters, and fans deserting the Tap ship like rats on the *Titanic*, Shrimpton, Tufnell, Smalls, Savage and St Hubbins decided to go on hiatus.

It would take a miracle for Tap to be in the same room together, let alone record together again. Thankfully, it was the '70s, miracles were easy to get hold of if you knew the right guys in the wrong places.

But no one, especially not the band, could predict that their particular miracle was going to be so nice, and so stinky, all at once…

TRACKLIST

1. 'Dancing Feet'
2. 'Knights Of The Round Turntable'
3. 'Eat The Beat'
4. 'Glamtasm'
5. 'Major Look, Major Stare'
6. 'Glitter And Gold'
7. 'Saturday Night Sweats'
8. 'Dance Off'
9. 'Hands In The Air'
10. 'Silent Disco'

Above: *In happier times, though not that you can tell from their faces.*

TAP UP CLOSE:
DEREK SMALLS

Bassist. Satanist. Christian. Art student. Pipe smoker. Prize-winning gardener. Jingle writer. Bitter divorcé. Internet addict. Zucchini smuggler. When it comes to being all these things, Derek Smalls is the only man you'll need (and find). As Tap's most level headed member – despite being much shorter than the rest of the band – Derek is the lukewarm water to David's fire and Nigel's ice, a role that is fairly fluid, allowing Derek the freedom to be non-committal to most things. Arise, Sir Smalls...

Derek Albion Smalls was born Derek Albion Smalls in Nilford-on-Null, in the West Midlands, in 1941. No one is quite sure when when, but his mother, Deidre, remembers he behaved "like a winter baby." Derek's father, Donald, or "Duff," had found a niche market of running an intermittently successful travelling telephone sanitization business, called Sani-Fone. During the band's hiatus in 1988, Derek returned to the UK to help run his father's business. "After a summer of sanitizing people's telephones you do appreciate rock 'n' roll a lot more," Derek said of this turbulent, but very hygienic, time.

A fan of rock 'n' roll from an early age, ("it's a great genre," he has said in multiple interviews) Derek learnt to play the bass guitar in 1958 (it was all the rage back then) when he enrolled at the London School of Design, aged 17. "Guitarists may have got all the girls, but bass playing was for the men," Derek has said. Indeed, during the band's 1988–1992 hiatus, Derek began a pet project that had been on his mind since his design school days: an album consisting entirely of music played on the bass. "The bass is a symbol, the basis of mankind. It just takes the idea of all bass as our base, is the fact that we are all people. Basses represent us," the bassist said during the time.

A self-trained bassist (and plumber, but that's not important), Derek first auditioned for the role of incoming Tap bass player in 1967, when outgoing Tap bassist Ronnie Pudding was dismissed by Nigel and Derek. Derek was a studio bassist, a job that required him turning up at various London studios with his bass and hoping someone needed a bass player, or at the very least a bass tuner. He had local success with his pre-Tap bands, Skaface (an all-white Jamaican band), Teddy Noise (where he developed his

"We've grown musically. Listen to some of the rubbish we did early on, it was stupid."

Derek Smalls

a love of loud music) and Milage whose first, and only, album *Milage 1*, Derek labelled, "A pre-Traffic Traffic. We had a flute player and a reed player, which was a bit much in the woodwind department."

Joining Tap in the middle of their ascension to fame – '(Listen to the) Flower People' was blowing up in many peoples' eardrums at the time – was a baptism of fire for Derek. As a Satanist and a Christian, this suited him fine and he coped very well. Spinal Tap's first tour around the "world and elsewhere" with Derek stage-right (audience, stage-left), proved to be a massive success (relative to the group's previous, and future, successes) and Derek's position in the band was secured.

As Derek's professional life bloomed, his personal life imploded. His marriage to Pamela Smalls was in the throes of a particularly ugly dissolution. His motto throughout this period was "Fuck my ex-wife's lawyer," a phrase that Nigel and David asked Derek to stop saying into the microphone onstage. In the divorce, Pamela got the Mini and the house, despite Derek's enquiries into having her "disappear." "I mean can't we have her killed?

You know people," he can be heard saying aloud to his lawyer in front of DiBergi's ever-present film crew during their "rockumentary," after news that their joint account had been used against him in his own divorce.

During the making of DiBergi's *This Is Spinal Tap* in 1982, it is perhaps Derek who fares the least well out of all the band members. Viewers will remember, in particular, the embarrassing incident passing through a metal detector at Chicago's O'Hare International Airport with a zucchini stuffed down his trousers ("it was there to improve my trouser thrust") as well the on stage incident stuck inside the alien pod during their performance of 'Rock 'n' Roll Creation.'

In 1988, following Tap's friendship hiatus, Derek remained in the music industry, albeit on the sidelines, when he joined a Christian heavy metal group called Lambsblood. The band recorded a few songs, including 'Job: What a Bloke' and 'Whole Lotta Lord,' and also appeared first on the bill at 1989's Monsters of Jesus festival. They split up shortly after, citing "irreconcilable dogmatic differences."

Author's note: *"Derek's lawyer has informed me to say that Derek still has the deepest respect and gratitude for the staff of Chicago's Transport Security Agency."*

"A man's relationship with the Devil is a very private affair."

Derek Smalls

THE GOSPEL ACCORDING TO TAP (OR ROCK 'N' ROLL CREATION) (1977)

Following the ill-conceived, ill-executed and ill-looking disco direction of 1976's *Tap Dancing*, the group desperately needed to revive their fortunes, friendship, reputation and bank balances. They had only one option: Go religious. God would forgive them if they failed, but could they forgive themselves if they didn't try to extend their fan base?

Above: *Tap move in mysterious ways, like God, their new muse.*
Opposite: *The Ten Commandments, according to Tap.*

On the tracklisting to 1975's triple live album *Jap Habit*, there was a song – a throwaway, a little ditty written by Nigel – something he had penned as part of his ongoing Mach compositions, but had a rocking hook that David and Derek thought was wasted on piano. The song was called 'Nice 'N Stinky.' And it was the miracle Spinal Tap needed, and the one that I mentioned on page 59.

Having not spoken to each other in almost four months, licking their individual wounds at home in England, Faith, Tufnel, Smalls and St Hubbins met at the Bucket (now the Bucket and Pail) on Squatney Road, Squatney (now Squatney-near-Thames) the first pub the band ever played, to discuss their future. However, manager Ian had some good news. It appeared 'Nice 'N Stinky' had become a big hit on the club scene in the US. The band's fans still wanted the Tap to continue to flow like the foursome faucet they were, despite the critical and commercial drubbing of *Tap Dancing*.

In the winter of 77, 'Nice N Stinky' was hovering in the Top 50 *Billboard* chart, but come the Summer it was inserting itself into the high teens (figuratively, not literally) where it stayed until autumn. The track's success generated some much-needed revenue for the group, which they promptly used to record their next album, *The Gospel According to Tap*, the band's swansong, and parting gift, to Megaphone. The label was gearing up to file several lawsuits against the band, many of which have still not been resolved, due to the band's legal representation moving addresses frequently to avoid subpoenas.

The Gospel According to Tap was again not a critical success. The album's heavy metal tunes with religious themes took a beating from all sides, with even the *Jewish Chronicle* weighing in: "Oh Vey!" the review's headline began, before concluding: "Schlocky songs by a bunch of schlemiels, shmucks and schmendriks with shlimazel." Another review, which was plastered on inside music magazine *MNE*, and famously brought to the band's attention for the first time in DiBergi's "rockumentary," highlights just how far removed the band had become from their own press: It read: "This pretentious ponderous collection of religious rock psalms is enough to prompt the question, 'What day did the Lord create Spinal Tap, and couldn't he have rested on that day too?'"

The album's rarely performed punk song, 'Young, Smug and Famous,' with its one chord, and sarcastic refrain of "I want to be young, smug and famous," reeked of desperation from a band approaching their 40s. "The song's a statement about young people who get everything they want. We're not jealous of them, we're just asking why them, and not us?" David remembered.

The band would later concede that *The Gospel According to Tap* had been "underlooked, underbought and under-recorded," prompting Megaphone A&R executive, Roger Felchstein to announce, "*The Gospel According to Tap* is our final release with England's so-

TAP'S TEN ROCK 'N' ROLL COMMANDMENTS

I

Rock 'n' roll keeps you young...
but you die young

II

Don't covet thy neighbour's guitar

III

If it's too loud, you're too close

IV

If you can read this, you're too close

V

There are no more commandments

VI

Memorize previous commandments

called loudest band. We wish them well, in so much that we hope they all fall down one and are never heard from again." "They were holding us back anyway," responded David politely, like the gentleman he is.

However, misery loves company and sad news once again knocks the band for six. Long-time drummer Peter "James" Bond also leaves the band for good. Though the circumstances of his departure remained unclear. All the band know is that he exploded in a ball of light while performing on stage at the Isle of Lucy Jazz-Blues Festival at Knotworthy Farm. Bond left without saying goodbye, which made it even worse for the band. "It was tragic really," recounted Nigel in DiBergi's 1982 "rockumentary." "He exploded on stage. He just was like a flash of green light...and that was it, nothing left. Well, there was a little green globule on his drum seat. It was a small stain actually." Bond's spontaneous combustion was devastating for Nigel: "For a drummer, he had very good time. He could actually keep the rhythm pretty much in the ballpark, as you would say, for the whole tune. His death really hit me the hardest, because he owed me money."

But every cloud has a silver lining. It was at the the wake of Bond, that David met future wife and

enthusiastic sexual partner Jeanine Pettibone. The couple would become one of rock 'n' roll's least talked about relationships.

It was during *Gospel's...* mini world tour around Scotland, that Tap – flushed with the cash from 'Nice 'N Stinky' – began introducing pyrotechnics and props on stage. Their most famous stage device, aside from the mini-Stonehenge, was Jim, the large skull which became a fully-fledged member of the band in 1992, Derek's dual-necked bass guitar, and the alien chrysalis pods which Derek, Nigel and David emerged from before they ripped into 'Rock 'n' Creation.' Following the release of *This Is Spinal Tap* in 1984, Marty DiBergi was much-maligned (by the band) for highlighting the technical difficulties the three members had in getting out of the pods night after night while on tour.

To see out the year, Tap perform on ABC-TV variety show *The TV Show*. Backstage Nigel is introduced to Marty DiBergi, and the two begin discussing their mutual love of fish, as well as the idea of working together on a movie. DiBergi's pitch to Nigel was simple: to follow Spinal Tap around while on tour, an AAA insight into a hard-working rock band. Nigel liked the idea, and promised to pitch it to the band. "It sounded like a good idea at the time," Nigel mentioned to manager Ian Faith. "As long he doesn't make us out to be complete fucking wankers."

Without a record deal, and their latest album underperforming, the band entered a phase of arrested development and briefly went their separate ways.

TRACKLIST

1. 'Young, Smug and Famous'
2. 'Rock 'N' Roll Creation'
3. 'Kaned and Abled'
4. 'Let There Be Dark'
5. 'Flock of Sheep'
6. 'No Room At The Inn'
7. 'Shepherd's Pie'
8. 'The First Christmas'
9. 'Holy Threesome (Father, Son and Holy Ghost)'
10. 'The Devil's In Me (Trying To Get Out)'
11. 'Good God'
12. 'One Myrrh Time'

"I'D SAY 80 PER CENT OF THE TIME, WELL, 70 PER CENT OF THE TIME, WELL, OK, 60 PER CENT OF THE TIME, DEREK GOT OUT OF THAT POD DURING 'ROCK 'N' ROLL CREATION' PERFECTLY OK. COUPLE OF TIMES IT DOESN'T OPEN AND DIBERGI PUTS THAT IN THE FILM. WHY DOES HE USE THAT BIT?"

DAVID ST HUBBINS

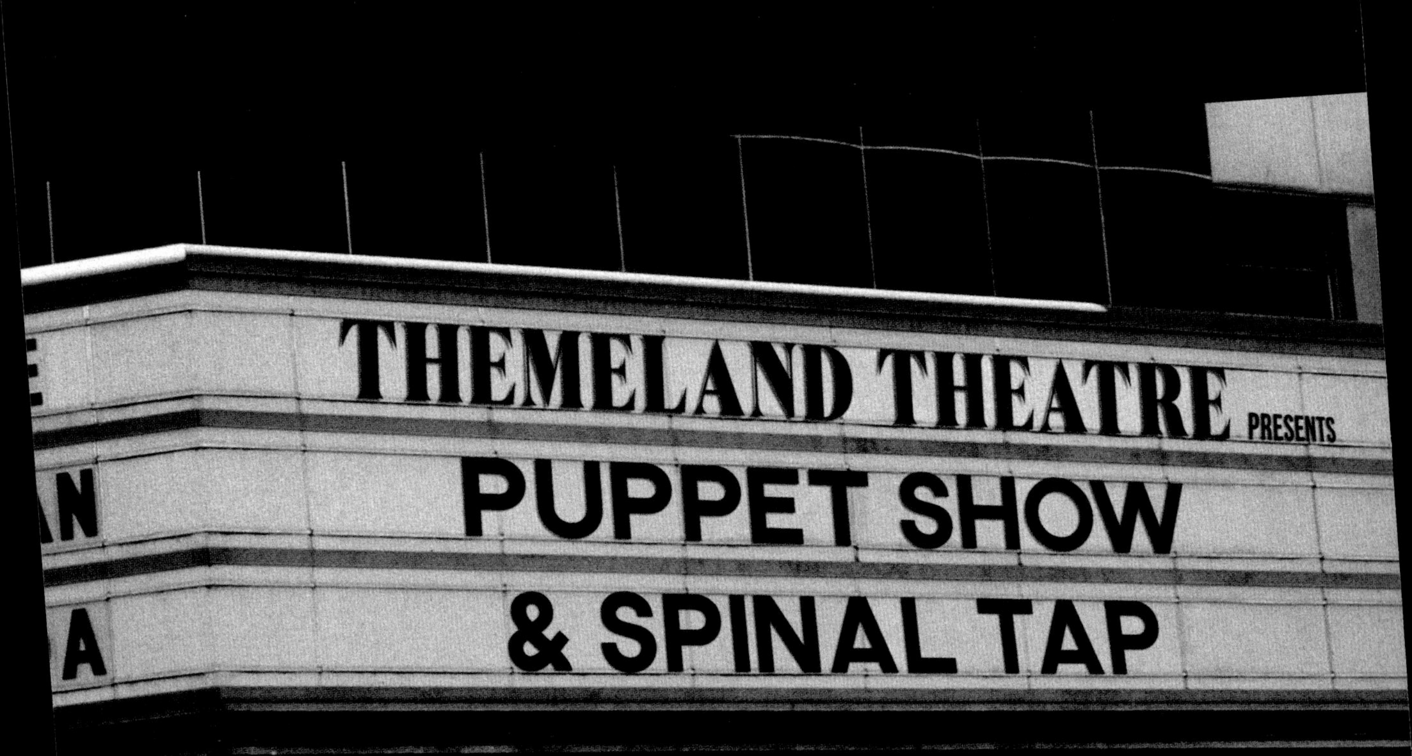
THEMELAND THEATRE PRESENTS
PUPPET SHOW
& SPINAL TAP

"WE'VE GOT A BIGGER DRESSING ROOM THAN THE PUPPETS? OH, THAT'S REFRESHING."

DAVID ST HUBBINS

THOSE THAT WERE THERE: JEANINE PETTIBONE

Despite 1982's *Smell the Glove* tour erupting into chaos before it started, it wasn't until the arrival of Jeanine Pettibone on "Visitor's Day" that the proverbial excrement to hit the metaphorical fan causing a symbolic wall to be parabolically pebbledashed with decorative liquid faeces. Put simply: her arrival caused a shit show.

In 1977, David met Jeanine Pettibone, his future second wife, following the divorce to his first chronological wife, Pamela. It was love at first sight, and a love that David has admitted candidly, and publicly, that he needed desperately. "Before I met Jeanine, my life was cosmically in shambles, he told DiBergi's camera during the 1982 filming of 1984's *This Is Spinal Tap*. He continued: "I was using bits and pieces of whatever Eastern philosophies happened to drift through my transom and she sort of sorted it out for me, straightened it out for me, gave me a path to follow." Jeanine introduced David to the ways of astral telepathy and writing his own horoscopes, as well as some out-there ideas about dressing the band up as Zodiac animals. "It's a way to fight the drabs. You know we've got the drabs," David reasoned with his bandmates, but the idea fell on deaf ears.

Jeanine's idea of giving the band "a new presentation," divided the group into two. Those who thought the idea was terrible, and David and Jeanine. "Can I have the floor for just one moment because I've got something I'd like to show you," David informed the group. "Jeanine's been working on these very hard. These are a new direction...a stage look...for the band fashioned after the signs of the zodiac." Unfortunately, this prompted cat-calls from the rest of the band, wondering if it was a joke. As always, it was the level-headed emotional intelligence of the band's resident Satanist that diffused the situation. "David, there are solutions to all problems," Derek interjected. "We can take the rational approach; we can say…" however Derek was interrupted by Nigel before he could ever finish his sentence. Thankfully, Nigel's suggestion was recreating Stonehenge on stage for their "druid pop song" 'Stonehenge.' A good idea – what could possibly

Above: *David's lookalike, and lover, Jeanine Pettibone.*

go wrong? – and all talk of zodiac animal costumes were instantly disregarded.

After having been appointed manager, following Ian Faith's sudden departure, Jeanine had grand designs on how to get the band back on track. "I care what happens to the band," she told Marty DiBergi, and explained how she was often an influential sounding board for David's musical expressions. "Oh, yeah, I mean, I listen to him when he's experimenting, and things like that. He plays things to me, sometimes when he's worked up, and he's got a new bit he wants to tell me about, you know, and I say 'Yeah, that's good,' or 'that's bad,' or 'that's shit' or whatever, you know." "Yes, she is very honest," agreed

"You don't get an audience if you don't have the stars and planets in alignment."

Jeanine Pettibone

David. "She gives me the brutally frank version and I sort of tart it up for the rest of the band."

A former tambourinist, Jeanine's firm appraisal of David, and the group at large, made her the worthy successor to Ian, dispensing practical advice to the band 24 hours a day: "She says she can hear that I'm eating too much sugar on the phone. She says my larynx is fat," David informs his bandmates, as captured by DiBergi's film crew. It is isn't just David who receives the sharp end of Jeanine's infinite wisdom. During one fraught discussion with Nigel, Jeanine bemoans the lack of production nous on *Smell the Glove*. "You know, it might have been better if the album had been mixed right. It wasn't. It was mixed all wrong, wasn't it? You couldn't hear the lyrics all over it. You don't do heavy metal in Doubly, you know." Sadly, Jeanine's mispronouncation of "Dolby" (all the rage back then) caused hysterics among the band, particularly Nigel, who used it as a way of using her managerial and musical inexperience against her ability to make sound judgment calls for the benefit of the band.

At the airport en route to Denver's $300-an-hour Rainbow Trout Studio to record guitar parts for the song 'America,' Jeanine announced to the group that her belief in the zodiac is what will save the band from further spiralling downwards into the absyss. "The band's sign is Virgo, and we see it's Saturn in the third, alright, and it is a bit rocky. But because Virgo is one of the most highly intelligent signs of the zodiac, we're gonna pull through this, with great aplomb." However, it is merely Jeanine's constant presence both in the studio and backstage that causes Nigel to lose his cool with his bandmates after David's apparent distraction from recording a guitar part correctly. "He can't play the fucking guitar anymore," Nigel bursts out loud, insulting David. "You can't fucking concentrate, because of your fucking wife, alright, it's your fucking wife!"

Following Jeanine's swift reorganization of a gig at Lindfield Air Base, Nigel leaves the band, forcing the group to abandon their setlist and dive headfirst into a free-form version of 'Jazz Odyssey,' a song that Derek had barely written, let alone wrote down. "You are witnesess at the new birth of Spinal Tap Mark II, hope you enjoy our new direction," Derek told 300 sleepy soldiers, after their relaxed At Ease weekend festivities.

David and Jeanine married in 1986 and consummated their marriage, which resulted in a son, Misha. They divorced in 2000, but remain on friendly terms for the sake of their respective karmas.

"HILARIOUS... SENDS UP WHAT THE BEATLES STARTED WITH 'A HARD DAYS NIGHT.'"
Bruce Williamson—Playboy

"DON'T MISS IT... ONE OF THE FUNNIEST MOVIES"
Stephen Shaefer—US Magazine

THIS IS

Spinal Tap

STARRING CHRISTOPHER GUEST · MICHAEL McKEAN · HARRY SHEARER · ROB REINER
JUNE CHADWICK · TONY HENDRA & BRUNO KIRBY   PRODUCED BY KAREN MURPHY
WRITTEN BY CHRISTOPHER GUEST & MICHAEL McKEAN & ROB REINER & HARRY SHEARER   DIRECTED BY ROB REINER

MIDDLEWORD

The past has passed.

The passed has past?

That's confusing, innit?

It's a good thing nobody asked me to write this book!

The point is: what more can be written about Spinal Tap that hasn't already been written?

Looking backwards is only good for two things: shouting at the drummer and parallel parking.

But seriously, it's nice that Wallace has written this lovely book about us, especially as it has so many pictures which makes it easy to just flick through quickly, and not dwell on specific incidents.

As for me, I can't remember very much about anything, really. I blame the Spandex, it restricted the blood flow upwards. I don't even remember when the '70s or '80s were, let alone what happened, so consider this a reliable record of events, even if it most definitely isn't.

Anyway, me, Derek and David (and all the others) have had a great laugh sucking on the sweet teat of rock 'n' roll and we owe it all to you loonies. Thanks for sticking with us for all these years, but especially 1971–72, 76–77, 79–80, 82–84 and 90–93.

Just to clarify: We're not dead. We're still all very much alive. No matter what the press writes.

New album out soon!

Lots of love,

Nigel

THE 1980s:
THE FALL OF TAP?

After the super-prolific, but mega-tumultuous, era that defined the 1970s, the next decade along chronologically – the 1980s – saw the band spiral further into disarray. The final straw in the camel that broke the coffin's back was the 1982 filming, and 1984 release, of Marty DiBergi's "rockumentary" with a motive, *This Is Spinal Tap*.

As 1979 drew to a whimpering close with Megaphone, 1980 opened with a bang with Polymer records. To celebrate Tap's new recording contract – it was touch and go for a while if they would ever be signed again – the band released one of their most confused albums, *Shark Sandwich*. While critics weren't kind to the album ("Shit Sandwich," being one review, the least venomous, actually), Tapheads lapped it up. The album contained the track 'Sex Farm,' which provided their fans with some sense of musical growth since 'Big Bottom,' even if the growth was more outward than upward.

Shit Sandwich, sorry *Shark Sandwich*'s, semi-success in Europe, North America and Japan (Kyoto only) allowed Tap the opportunity to Tap into America for a 1984 tour and another album, *Smell the Glove*. It was following the recording and release of this album that the band fell further into chaos. It was Polymer's immediate unhappiness with the "offensive" and "sexist" album cover ("a greased, naked woman on all fours with a dog collar around her neck and a leash and a man's arm extended out holding onto the leash and pushing a black glove into her face, to sniff it") that led to the release of the record with a "none more black" cover after, as Ian explained to the group, "experimenting with packaging materials." As Bobbi Flekman explained: "Money talks and bullshit walks. If the first album was a hit then we could have pressed on Polymer to release the album as it was, but it wasn't."

In retaliation to the label's claims about the band's choice of artwork, David remained prickly when Polymer's PR "hostest with the mostest" Bobbi Flekman confronted them about the label's position at the album's New York launch. "You know, if we were serious and we said, 'Yes, she should be forced to smell the glove,' then

"The '80s were a blur, really. And not just because I lost my glasses."

Nigel Tufnel

you'd have a point, but it's all a joke." However, David's succinct point was lost when Nigel chimed in, confusing the band's position on whether it was a joke or not, when he exclaimed: "It is and it isn't. She should be made to smell it, but not, you know, over and over."

While manager Ian Faith did his best to defuse the band's anger (it's "simple, beautiful, classic,") the rest

Opposite: *Tap's most beloved groupie, Brinke Stevens, shares her duties with a friend.*
Above: *Derek, Nigel and David practice the Tap pout.*

of the band, who had poured considerable blood, tears, and semen, into deciding the album design, concluded that the final release, a jet black cover treatment, was nothing more than "a black mirror" (Nigel) and "looks like death" (David).

Towards the end of the calamitous 1982 *Smell the Glove* tour, Ian, Nigel and Mick Shrimpton all left the band. Ian "the other dead man," as David began to refer to him, took a forced hiatus after the remaining members undermined his authority and replaced him with the Tap's tambourinist, Jeanine. Ian quit after refusing to work alongside Jeanine, storming out in a rage, shouting, "I am not managing them with you or any other woman ... especially one that dresses like an Australian's nightmare. So fuck you!" Following this outburst, Nigel left the band after refusing to play Lindberg Air Force base, leaving the band in chaos as to how to play his parts, a solution which unfolded unprofessionally at their next gig at Stockton's Themeland, where they were supported by a Puppet Show. Nigel's departure was a shock to Marty DiBergi, who caught the trio of disasters – Ian's walkout, Nigel's walkout and Mick's explosion – on camera. The

director exclaimed: "I can't believe it. I can't believe it, that, you're lumping Nigel in with these people you've played with for a short period of time." David remained resolute on Nigel's swift exit: "No, we shan't work together again."

Released in March 1984, *This Is Spinal Tap*, the defining warts-(and herpes)-and-all tour film ever made, disappeared without much a fuss. Its failure in the theatres was matched only by its success on home videos, prompting the band to put down their instruments and go on an eight-year-long hiatus, which produced smatterings of solo musical efforts, but more of a focus on family: Derek went home to Nulford-on-the-Nil, Nigel became an inventor, and David taught soccer in California.

This cruel decade ended in triumph, however. In 1990, Ian Faith "died." His "death" bought the band back together, who regrouped for 1992's *Break Like the Wind*. Sadly, rumours of Ian's death were greatly exaggerated – despite the band dancing on his grave merrily. Ian was alive and well. But who cares? The band were back together, just as the 1990s party was getting started…

"It's 1982, get out of the '60s, we don't have this mentality anymore."

Bobbi Flekman, on *Smell the Glove*

"WELL, IT'S ONE LOUDER, ISN'T IT? IT'S NOT TEN. YOU SEE, MOST BLOKES, YOU KNOW, WILL BE PLAYING AT TEN. YOU'RE ON TEN HERE, ALL THE WAY UP, ALL THE WAY UP, ALL THE WAY UP, YOU'RE ON TEN ON YOUR GUITAR. WHERE CAN YOU GO FROM THERE? WHERE?"

NIGEL TUFNEL

"NOW, I MEAN TAKING A SONG LIKE 'SEX FARM,' WE'VE TAKEN THE SOPHISTICATED VIEW OF THE IDEA OF SEX AND MUSIC AND PUT IT ON A FARM."

DEREK SMALLS

SHARK SANDWICH (1980)

Spinal Tap's first album with Polymer Records, was hoping to be a successful 'comeback' following the bad smells that had followed the band since *Tap Dancing*. Sadly, the album's reviews were "not good," and neither were the sales. Undeterred by failure, Tap limped on…the band are nothing if not persistent.

Following their "sudden and immediate" release from their Megaphone contract, Spinal Tap were homeless label-wise for several months. Thankfully, the band's British accents paid off when Polymer Records chairman Sir Denis Eton-Hogg, another limey in America, wanted to help out his fellow countrymen and offer them a two-album deal on the condition that they were granted absolutely no power whatsoever contractually when it came to their music, album covers or touring itinerary. Ian Faith, knowing that this was the best offered they'd get, took it gladly.

Picking up with their heavy metal sound where they left it a few years earlier, Tap believed that a new label, a new tour and their old sound, their fans would return en masse. They were half wrong. *Shark Sandwich* received mixed reviews, one famous one, read out by DiBergi in his "rocumentary" to all-round embarrassment by the band, simply read: "Shit Sandwich." Of course, this was not the band's only two-word review in their career, having previously been described live as "Spinal Crap." Defensive, David rubbished the record's reviews, especially regarding the album's cover: "We have too much raw energy to be captured on the cold surface of a CD," he said. "If you truly want to experience Tap at work, come to our shows. Playing live is our bread and butter. The stage is where we eat and our music is a feast for the eyes, ears, intestines and swimsuit area."

The album, hampered by Polymer's disastrous promotion attempt that involved sending actual shark-fin sandwiches to reviewers, an idea suggested by Bobbi Flekman, the chain-smoking artist relations officer for Polymer Records and who was stuck in charge of Tap's PR presence during the early 1980s. None of the band had a good word to say about Flekman, but perhaps Nigel summed her up best: "If she hadn't been a cheat, a liar and a bitch, she would have been a great girl."

Shark Sandwich – so named because sharks were all the rage in the '80s, and following the release of great white horror shark movie *Big Teeth* in 1975 – is a veritable feast of music *and* lyrics, with the nihilistic dungeon-rocker 'No Place Like Nowhere,' the disco-raver 'Throb Detector' (a song they recorded for *Tap Dancing*, but excluded it for being "too shit" for that album but then included for *Shark Sandwich* because "we needed filler; we hadn't written enough songs," said Derek). Of course, despite the album's critical

"The review you had on *Shark Sandwich* … which was merely a two word review – just said 'Shit Sandwich.'"

Marty DiBergi

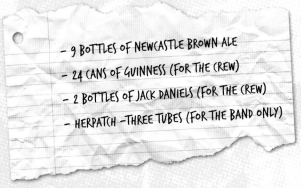

- 9 BOTTLES OF NEWCASTLE BROWN ALE
- 24 CANS OF GUINNESS (FOR THE CREW)
- 2 BOTTLES OF JACK DANIELS (FOR THE CREW)
- HERPATCH – THREE TUBES (FOR THE BAND ONLY)

Above: *Band rider, 1980.* **Opposite:** *Tap with Polymer's Denis Eton-Hogg.*

TRACKLIST

1. 'No Place Like Nowhere'
2. 'Throb Detector'
3. 'Sex Farm'
4. 'This Way Up (But The Other Way Round)'
5. 'Back Alley Sally'
6. 'Mental In The Mind'
7. 'Choking Hazard'
8. 'Ribbed For Pleasure'
9. 'Cock Fight'

mauling, there was a few positives to take away from the album. The monster success of 'Sex Farm,' may have been reviewed as an "immature, innuendo-driven dirge of tasteless lyrics," but most reviews confessed that it was a "teenage boys' wet dream," and subsequently gave Tap their fifth proper US 'hit' single, sliding in easily at No.32 on the *Billboard* chart. The song's success gave Polymer some confidence that signing Tap was not that big of a mistake. To take advantage of the band's North American success, Polymer gave Tap a hefty three-figure album advance to record their next album, the "semenal" (not my word) *Smell the Glove*.

Derek considers *Shark Sandwich* one of his favourite Tap albums. "It's close to my heart," he said, during an interview in 1981, "because I snuck into the mixing studio after the other lads had left and turned up my bass part." This would explain the very heavy and loud bass mix on the album's production.

Shark Sandwich's literal album cover – shark fins emerging out of the top slice of what appears to be a nutritionally valueless white-bread sandwich – was designed by famous '70s album heavy metal cover artist, Rock Stromthorn. "I don't remember doing this album at all," Stromthorn remembers. "The cover is pretty unimaginative, a literal description of the title, so they must have not paid me very much to do it. It was probably a morning's work."

With *Shark Sandwich* treading water commercially and the band unable to float without armbands, the beginning of the 1980s had so far yet to be kind to the group. Creative differences between Nigel and David – usually closer than brothers – had started to show cracks. David and Jeanine's relationship, which began at

Bond's wake, had flourished and became rather intense, pushing Nigel and David's friendship to the sidelines.

With *Shark Sandwich*, Spinal Tap had released yet another album that had failed to set the world alight. (Derek blamed the album's production: "The bass is too loud," while adding, confused: "Our songs were big, fat analog sounds, these weren't digital sounds, and the digital machines try to interpret them and they go, 'Wait a minute, that's a one and it's a zero,' and the whole thing breaks down.")

However, not all was lost out at sea, Nigel's chance encounter with filmmaker, and fan, Marty DiBergi in 1978 was now about to give Tap yet another opportunity to waltz back into the spotlight...

"YOU PLAY TO A PREDOMINANTLY WHITE AUDIENCE. DO YOU FEEL YOUR MUSIC IS RACIST IN ANY WAY?"

MARTY DIBERGI

SMELL THE GLOVE (1982)

The band's fifteenth album, and second (and final) album for Polymer Records before going on extended hiatus, was a critical disaster, with many reviews appalled by the obvious lack of musical direction of the songs, not to mention the controversy over the cover. But England's loudest band were never going to be silenced by their critics, only their fans could do that. And as long as the band's loyal Tapheads grew to love the album, that's all that mattered. That and royalties.

Before the release of *Smell the Glove* – gloves were all the rage as the 'must-have accessory' of the early 1980s – Ian Faith had managed to secure a North American tour to promote the album many (but not all) members of Spinal Tap were claiming was the group's best record ever. The tour was signed off by Polymer's chairman, Denis Eton Hogg, when it was announced that filmmaker Marty DiBergi would join the band to capture the sights, "the sounds and the smells, of a hard-working rock band on the road," on the band's first North American tour in six years.

When Polymer promoter Bobbi Flekman told the band that their album cover for their latest release, *Smell the Glove* was "sexist," Ian Faith, David, Nigel and Derek were initially not horrified. When they later found out she said "sex-*ist*," and not "sexy," the band were horrified. But not because the album cover *was* actually sex*ist* – it was 1982, sexism was en vogue, everyone was doing it – but because they for once could

not get their own way.

As a compromise, to help suite the demands of retailers such as Sears and Kmart (who were refusing to stock the album with the original artwork) the band were forced to release the album with a "none more black" cover that neither expressed the sexuality of the music encased within, nor the growth of sexual maturity of the group's members. This was the band's most sexually mature album to date – gone were the days of 'Lick My Love Pump,' 'Hell Hole,' 'Big Bottom,' 'Nice and Stinky,' 'Swallow My Love,' 'Lie Back and Take It,' 'Throb Detector,' 'Sex Farm' and 'Saucy Jack' and many

The pair of gloves used on the cover, on display in Hard Rock Cafe, Luxembourg.

Left: *Viv and Nigel deep-ish in conversation.*

Opposite above: *The final packaged edition of* Smell the Glove.

Opposite below: *Band rider, 1982.*

"You should have seen the cover they *wanted* to do. It wasn't a glove, believe me."

Ian Faith

- I CASE OF DR PEPPER (FOR THE BAND)
- 10 CASES OF COORS (FOR THE CREW)
- ASSORTED DELI PLATTERS
- A SELECTION OF BEEF STICKS
- CHEESEBALLS AND SHERRIED CLAM PUFFS ON A CRYSTAL SERVER
- 48 MR GOODBARS - WITH THE NUTS REMOVED
- MENDOCINO ROCKET FUEL (VIV TO SOURCE?)

more – *Smell the Glove* was instead full of much more lyrical diversity and used chords that were a stretch not only for the band's fingers, but also for their minds.

Released in 1982, a year that also saw the release of Terry Ladd's Duke Fame's mega-successful single 'Wet 'N Wild' and the platinum-selling album, *Rock Hard*. As Tap's archenemy, Ladd's success did nothing but make the band eager to get back to where they had been during their Thamesmen days. *Smell the Glove*, a "turning point" for the band, as Ian freely admits, was "a make or break" recording that could see the group return to their glory days.

TRACKLIST

1. 'Hell Hole'
2. 'Smell the Glove'
3. 'Polly Polygamy'
4. 'Lightening Rod'
5. 'Open Wide'
6. 'No Need for That'
7. 'Pull The Other One'
8. 'Leather Interior'
9. 'Two Hands Required'
10. 'Beef Jerky'

"The last time Tap toured America, they were, uh, booked into 10,000 seat arenas, and 15,000 seat venues, and it seems that now, on their current tour they're being booked into 1,200 seat arenas, 1,500 seat arenas, and uh I was just wondering, does this mean uh … the popularity of the group is waning?"

Marty DiBergi

After seeing the "Black Album," as it went on to become known by loyal fans, for the first time in Milwaukee during a sound check, the band's disappointment was obvious. "This is something you put around your arm. You don't put this on your fucking turntable," David exclaimed, angrily.

The cover may have caused controversy, but the music spinning inside it, decidedly lacked all controversy. Containing only two singles, 'Hell Hole' and 'Pull The Other One' *Smell the Glove* made a splash upon its release in the US charts at No.69, the band's lowest ever chart placement, causing Derek, Nigel and David to put a hold on all touring commitments past 1984. Many shows had thankfully been cancelled anyway, due to various still "unspecified reasons." The band returned despondently to England to lick their wounds. They would not be seen again until 1992 for *Break Like the Wind*, a return to their old-school "sexy" sound, not heard since 1974's *Intravenus de Milo*.

Thanks to DiBergi's "rockumentary" film crew

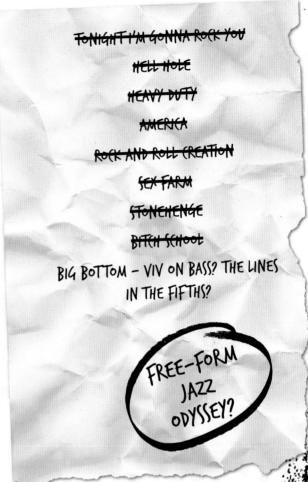

lurking forever in the backgroud capturing every slice
of foldable bread, Tap were now closer to the abyss
than ever before. *Smell the Glove* had left a bad taste in
Polymer's mouth, and after only two albums, decided
to pull out and wipe itself clean from the skidmarks of
association left by Spinal Tap.

Above: *The original cover of*
Smell the Glove.

Above right: *Setlist from
the ill-fated Lindberg Air
Base concert.*

TONIGHT I'M GONNA ROCK YOU

HELL HOLE

HEAVY DUTY

AMERICA

ROCK AND ROLL CREATION

SEX FARM

STONEHENGE

BITCH SCHOOL

BIG BOTTOM – VIV ON BASS? THE LINES
IN THE FIFTHS?

FREE-FORM
JAZZ
ODYSSEY?

"You put a greased naked woman on all fours with a dog collar around her neck, and a leash, and a man's arm extended out up to here, holding onto the leash, and pushing a black glove in her face to sniff it. You don't find that offensive? You don't find that sexist?" Bobbi Flekman

TAP INTO AMERICA

Onstage disasters, spontaneous combustions, getting lost backstage, cancelled gigs, bad reviews, bizarre gardening accidents, the curious relocation of cold sores, onstage prop-related mishaps and, well, you get the picture, 1984 was the year that tits went up, down and sideways for the band. But this is Spinal Tap… they won't go down unless they really, really, have to.

In 1984 George Orwell fans celebrated the eighty-first anniversary of the famed author's death, and the same year also marked the release of Marty DiBergi's dreadful tour "rockumentary" about the band, *This Is Spinal Tap*. DiBergi and his film crew followed the band with Access All Area passes – which even some of the band were not allowed – on their 14-date North American tour across college towns and mid-capacity arenas, capturing the group (perhaps too) up-close

and personal, in the hope of depicting what life is like on the road for an ageing band whose career is, quite visibly, about to be thrown under the tour bus.

To celebrate the film's complete failure in theatres, let's take a look at the quotations that were most taken out of context by Marty DiBergi, and used as propaganda by critics to slander the career of a band who had done nothing but defy the law of averages to be a success. Shame on you, DiBergi…

"It's part of a trilogy, a musical trilogy I'm working on in D minor which is the saddest of all keys, I find. People weep instantly when they hear it, and I don't know why."

Nigel Tufnel

"I envy us."

David St Hubbins

"You'd like bigger bread?"

Ian Faith

"Well, I'm sure I'd feel much worse if I weren't under such heavy sedation."

David St Hubbins

"We're anything but racists."

Nigel Tufnel

"This miniature bread. I've been working with this now for about half an hour and I can't figure it out..."

Nigel Tufnel

A[...] [...]s large Scottish home, purchased as a possible tax write-off, is known to locals as "the Ruin."

"That's not to say I haven't had my visionary moments. I've taken acid 75, 76 times."

Derek Smalls

"A jog? We don't have time for that."

Derek Smalls

"I'm tired of sticking up for his intelligence."

David St Hubbins, on Nigel

"IT'S NOT GOING TO AFFECT MY PERFORMANCE, DON'T WORRY ABOUT THAT. I JUST HATE IT ... IT REALLY, IT DOES DISTURB ME, BUT I'LL RISE ABOVE IT; I'M A PROFESSIONAL."

NIGEL TUFNEL

THOSE THAT WERE THERE: MARTY DiBERGI

Marty "the butcher" DiBergi. One of Spinal Tap's earliest fans was also the chief architect responsible for bringing down his idols with his lazy and poorly edited "rockumentary" *This Is Spinal Tap*. A commercial flop on release, but a stiff success in the burgeoning home video VHS market (that was all the rage back then), the movie was to make fools of Spinal Tap, despite their years of hard work cultivating a professional, and punctual, reputation.

What should have been a perfume-spritzed love letter to his favourite band, ended up being an anthrax-laced parcel of dog shit. Marty DiBergi's 1984 "horror film" began sincerely enough, with the filmmaker gleefully describing the honour of working so closely with a band he clearly adored. "In the late fall of 1982 when I heard that Tap was releasing a new album called *Smell the Glove*, and was planning their first tour of the United States in almost six years to promote that album. I jumped at the chance to make the documentary, the, if you will, rockumentary that you're about to see. I wanted to capture the sights, the sounds, the smells, of a hard-working rock band on the road. And I got that. But I got more, a lot more."

What does he mean he got a "lot more"? And if he did have loads more why didn't he use it, because the film is only 85 minutes long – plenty of time to squeeze in footage of when the band managed to walk to the stage without getting lost, or successfully getting out of the "Creation" pods, and shows that weren't cancelled due to advertising funds, or gigs where power failures did not halt the performance, or guitar solos that didn't require the assistance of a roadie to help pick Nigel up off the stage floor or shows where they headlined *above*

Above: *"I hated that fucking stupid hat," said Derek.*
Opposite: *Viv tells DiBergi about his love of video games.*

"I'm a film maker. I make a lot of commercials. That little dog that chases the covered wagon underneath the sink? That was mine."

Marty DiBergi

"I just tried to show them in a good light, to make them more human."

Marty DiBergi

Puppet Shows. Surely, there was plenty of this footage that existed that he could have shown, but didn't. Why?

It was in 1966 that DiBergi first tasted the delicious umami taste of Spinal Tap's haute cuisine. The young student had gone to New York's Electric Banana in Greenwich to watch the Thamesmen perform their successful double A-side single 'Cups and Cakes' / 'Gimme Some Money.' There was also an all-you-can-eat buffet at the gig, but that was just a bonus. "In 1966, I went down to Greenwich Village, New York City to a rock club called the Electric Banana. Don't look for it, it's not there anymore." DiBergi told the audience at the start of his "rockumentary." "The gig was the best show I ever saw. Plus, the buffet shrimp was delicious," he later announced in an interview, amidst accusations that he "stitched up" the group, accusations he has denied vehemently. "I have nothing but enduring love for England's loudest band," he said.

Since the release, and countless re-releases of *This Is Spinal Tap* on home video formats (all the rage in the 80s), DiBergi has slipped into relative obscurity, having not made a movie since *Toast!*, a straight-to-video film that is not worth going into detail here.

DiBergi, a filmmaker who made a seminal "rockumentary" about a hard-working rock band, or a bearded-faced liar who exploited his heroes for money? Only history is allowed the final say…

THIS IS SPINAL TAP

Marty DiBergi's 1984 "rockumentary" of Spinal Tap on their _Smell the Glove_ 1982 North American tour was meant to reinvigorate the band and set the ship straight after a few years of being lost at sea. However, DiBergi's "dreadful directing style" and "ridiculous editing" (Derek's words) and "terrible fashion choices" made the band look like a "bunch of plonkers" (most critics).

Described as a "horror film" by the entire band, their management, Polymer Records and many devoted fans, DiBergi's 'film' was the very antithesis of what the band yearned for. "After DiBergi's 'film' came out, we effectively did a lot of whingeing and moaning about it," said Derek. "We felt like he had stitched us up and made us out to look foolish. Bad things happen on a tour to every band, not just us. I guess, anyway. It's hard to tell what happens in other bands, when you're only in your own band."

Defending his film, DiBergi issued a statement: "I tried to show them in a good light. I wanted to make them look human." As DiBergi at the start of his "rockumentary" claims, he is one of the band's biggest fans, and turned down directing many major motion pictures in order to work so closely with the band, including _One Golden Pond – 3D_, and _Attack of the Full-Figured Gals_ – definite blockbusters.

Having met with Nigel in 1978 and exchanged napkins with phone numbers on, and promises to call one another's people, DiBergi was thrilled when Polymer approved the director's request to work with "England's loudest band." The subsequent "rockumentary" was intended to follow the band on their 14-date North American tour, travelling east to west, starting in New York (east) for an opening party and opening gig, and concluding in Los Angeles (west). Unfortunately, the band had been away from the US for six years. America had changed. A lot. It was now the 1980s. Fans now attended their shows in power suits, high on cocaine and CDO swaps. America had forgotten how to rock. While Ian Faith knew that Tap were never going to "saturate the New York market," where all the yuppies lived, he had faith that the shows would go down a treat in cities like Philadelphia, "real rock 'n' roll towns."

After a slow start in New York, meeting with Polymer staffers Bobbi Flekman and chairman Denis Eton-Hogg, the band discovered, from Flekman, that the album cover for _Smell the Glove_ had been "boycotted" by Sears and Kmart, two of the US's biggest music retailers. This news set in motion a chain of events (so believe David and Janine, whose astral projecting and zodiacal networking had begun to give them some clairvoyance) that the "the notion of a black album has really cursed us, in a way."

Cursed or not, DiBergi was there at every opportunity of the band's downward spiral from that point. From the non-adherence to the band's rider at the Vandermint Auditorum, North Carolina (the "miniature bread debacle,") where the band also kicked support band the Dose off the tour blaming the lead singer for the epidemic "outbreak of oral herpes simplex," to multiple gig cancellations, hotel room reservation "crossed wires" in Memphis, Derek getting stuck in an onstage pod prop, the departure of manager of Ian Faith, the appointment of Jeanine Pettibone as manager, the Themeland support slot to a puppet show, the departure and return of Nigel, and of course, the death of two more drummers.

All these moments were caught on film by DiBergi, and then edited together to make the band seem as if this tour was the tour from hell. "There were obviously loads of great things that happened too," said Nigel after watching the film. "I can't think of anything off the top of my head. Don't you hate it when that happens?"

"It was a real hatchet job," declared David. "What's bigger than a hatchet? A tomahawk?"

To the band's relief, _This Is Spinal Tap_ was a tremendous flop commercially when it was released theatrically. To the band's dismay, however, the movie was a hit in the burgeoning home video market (all the rage with coked-up yuppies), prompting the distributor to release the movie on multiple formats over multiple editions for the next 40 years. "Everywhere we go, this

"I wanted to capture the sights, the sounds, the smells, of a hard-working rock band on the road. And I got that. But I got more, a lot more."

Marty DiBergi

"'rockumentary' follows us around," says David. The film certainly made critics and fans remember who Spinal Tap were. "I do know that critics who used to pass us off as sort of a nobody band are beginning to re-emerge and, uh, say basically say the same thing," said David.

Thankfully, "the butcher DiBergi" (as the band now refer to him) has never worked in Hollywood, not even North Hollywood, ever again. He did direct a few straight-to-video movies, including *Kramer vs Kramer vs Godzilla, The Sleeping Policeman,* and *The Night of the Killer Carpet.* "Things have been going well for me," DiBergi claimed, when I visited his office to interview him, which was situated in a corridor next to a pay phone, the men's toilet and a water fountain.

The inevitable sequel to *This Is Spinal Tap*, 1992's *The Return of Spinal Tap* (what a lazy title!) was a cash-in by the band to promote their most recent album, *Break Like the Wind,* and shift stock from expensive rented warehouses. The film, directed by Jim DiBergi (not related), was a badly received concert film with behind-the-scenes footage, the only highlights being Nigel demonstrating his inventing nous with his Foldable Wine Glass™ and a skat-rap version of 'Sex Farm,' which made audiences yearn for the original. *The Return of Spinal Tap* is unavailable in many countries due to its "low level coarse language" and is for devoted Tapheads only.

Above: *DiBergi used comic books – the obsession of young American white boys – to promote* This is Spinal Tap *to the band's similar fanbase.*

"I BELIEVE VIRTUALLY EVERYTHING I READ. AND I THINK THAT IS WHAT MAKES ME MORE OF A SELECTIVE HUMAN THAN SOMEONE WHO DOESN'T BELIEVE ANYTHING."

DAVID ST HUBBINS

"DAVID, WE HAD A 15-YEAR RIDE, MATE. I MEAN, WHO WANTS TO BE A FUCKIN' 45-YEAR OLD ROCK 'N' ROLLER FARTING AROUND IN FRONT OF PEOPLE LESS THAN HALF THEIR AGE, CRANKING OUT SOME KIND OF MEDIOCRE HEAD-BANGING BULLSHIT, YOU KNOW, THAT WE'VE FORGOTTEN."

DEREK SMALLS

THE 1990s: LONG LIVE TAP

Shuffling slowly into the 1990s, Spinal Tap had enjoyed a six-year nap before the dawn of a new decade brought them back from the dead and desperate for money. The calamitous early 80s period of *This Is Spinal Tap* and *Smell the Glove* hadn't killed them off completely. They had one last trick hidden up their Spandex trousers…but would they dare pull it out?

Rock exile when you're aged over 40 is a tough place to live. No one knows you, your once-teenage fans have grown up, matured, and no longer think you're music is cool. You're an embarrassment, a has-been, no longer a gonna-be. For Spinal Tap, living in the wilderness of success, despite years of experience living there, hit them hard. But life in exile was twice as hard for Tap, because everything is. Their last album, *Smell the Glove*, was publically derided, and while it was all Polymer's fault, the group also had to suffer the ignominy of their album's failures being captured, and recorded, on film by DiBergi's documentary crew and then viewed by their own fans, fans who only wanted to watch their heroes fly high on the silver screen, a medium that had never experienced Tap before. The shame and ridicule bought on by the "rockumentary" was a double tap to the head, and Marty DiBergi was the trained killer who pulled the trigger.

Anyway, the band have asked me not to linger in the past. Their success lies in the future.

On November 12, 1990, Derek found out that Ian Faith, the band's former manager – who quit before the Japanese leg of the *Smell the Glove* tour, and replaced by Jeanine Pettibone – had "died"*. Cause of death? A suspected fatal cocktail of drugs following a three-week binge while having over-indulged while in residence at the Chelsea Hotel, New York. During the funeral, Derek, David and Nigel – who had not seen each in more than four years – caught up and rekindled their friendship while literally, and visibly, dancing on Ian's grave. While many onlookers first suspected the group were paying their last respects by stamping down dirt, it soon became apparent this was not the case when the trio became whooping, hollering, high-fiving and Nigel cheering, "Bye Ian! Come back as something I can eat." It was apparent that the group had not got over Ian's behaviour during the *Smell the Glove* tour, with his now-infamous tantrums and incompetence caught by DiBergi's camera. Believing Ian was dead and buried seemed as good a time as any to get the band back together. However, it wasn't until drummer Ric Shrimpton, Mick Shrimpton's younger brother (by 20 minutes), suggested that they regroup that the thought had even crossed their minds. "Hey, you guys should regroup," Ric told the trio, moments after they had been told to leave Ian's graveside.

And with that, Derek, David and Nigel, plus Ric, began rehearsing. Despite prompting the band

Left: *A wide selection of Tap toys are now available online to purchase. Which member will you play with?*

> ## "1984 was a bad year for music. But a worse year for us."
>
> ### Nigel Tufnell

to reunite, Ric was not made a member of the band until two years later, after undergoing a rigorous audition process. The band, who had already felt "sort of responsible" for the death of Mick, didn't want to be responsible for the death of a second Shrimpton.

Unfortunately, no other drummer wanted to join the band for fear of the Curse, so Ric was promptly hired on January 30, 1992, as tour drummer to support the group's new LP, *Break Like the Wind*. With the album out in the shops on March 17, and remaining in the shops unsold for several weeks, Spinal Tap did what they did best to support new music and make money. They went on tour. A ten-date tour of the UK, Sweden, Norway, Germany ensued, as did on-tour mishaps, proving that DiBergi's "rockumentary" was no fluke. Despite these accidents, or because of them, the group felt that they had to play Marty DiBergi at his own game and hired Jim DiBergi (no relation) to film *The Return of Spinal Tap* for a straight-to-home video movie, in order to whip up some promotion for the lacklustre album, ticket and merchandise sales for *Break Like the Wind*. For all of Jim DiBergi's film's faults, it at least threw a new spotlight on the band, giving Nigel and Derek a platform to promote their inventing accomplishments and helping secure patents for Nigel's Foldable Wine Glass™ and Derek's Death by Midnight™ black rose. Sadly, Jim DiBergi's documentary was also badly edited and, like Marty DiBergi's movie, made the group out to be a complete bunch of incompetent dildoes. "We got stiffed twice by the DiBergi family," Nigel said, who couldn't understand that Marty and Jim were not related.

When 1994 rolled around, Marty DiBergi – who was now in seriously dire financial straits – re-released *This Is Spinal Tap* for the first time. In the years since, the VHS and DVD edition of the film has been released scores of times, on multiple formats, much to the band's continuing horror.

Things started look up for the band in 1996, with the birth of the digital era. Several years before, Tim Berners-Lee, a fellow Englishman, had invented "the Internet."

Fellow inventor, Nigel, was impressed with the future possibilities of "the Internet" and acquired www.spinaltap.com from a US medical center (who specialized in Lumbar puncture procedures) for the sum of $50,000 dollars. The group's website went live a few days later and has remained unchanged, or updated, ever since.

With their 1992–1993 European tour a washout, *Break Like the Wind's* critical and commercial mauling and even more embarrassment on *The Return of Spinal Tap*, the nineties were about to become Spinal Tap's third least successful decade (out of four). From 1996–1999, the group returned to the shadows, awaiting for the next opportunity to flog a dead horse and continue tapping into the future. They wouldn't have to wait long. In 1999, while listening to the news on the radio in his car, David heard about about how the end of the world will happen at the stroke of midnight on January 31, 1999. The seemingly inevitable death, destruction and ruin of all mankind – just a few short months away – gave David an idea. Spinal Tap would, of course, go on to tour one last time before everybody on earth died. It would be the greatest tour of all time. They would call it 'Tap2K,' and at midnight on the final night of the tour, January 31, the band would explode in a climactic ball of flames along with their most loyal fans. Was this the end of Spinal Tap, and of all life on earth? Would Y2K kill us all?*

*No.

BREAK LIKE THE WIND (1992)

After an eight-year hiatus Spinal Tap defied all expectations and logic and regrouped. They also returned to the studio to record an album many wish they hadn't. With a UK tour in tow, *Break Like the Wind* breaks several of the band's previous sales records – lowest first day sales, lowest first week sales, and lowest overall sales. The band was back!

"It's a concept album," David told the gathered glitterati of the world's music press, on the day of *Break Like the Wind's* March 17, 1992 release. "And the concept is sales. It sounds crude, but it's part of our new maturity we find ourselves trapped in."

Following the release of "mature" lead single 'Bitch School,' which was itself accompanied by a "racy, but educational" music video directed by shock-filmmaker Artisan Wells. The song charted, but no one knows where, or how.

In the eight years that had elapsed between *Glove* and *Wind* the band had been relatively fallow. The band had announced they were "on hiatus," and were not pictured together again until 1991, outside of Rainbow Trout Studios, the only studio available at the time that would allow the reformed group to record.

In those wilderness years, David and Jeanine had married in 1986; Derek had formed his new Christian rock group Lambsblood; Nigel had become an inventor, and manager Ian Faith had "died" in 1990.

For the album, Tap regrouped – not because they wanted too. But because the brother of an old friend wanted them too. Ric Shrimpton, the younger brother (by 20 minutes) of Mick Shrimpton, the drummer who had exploded on stage during Tap's previous comeback tour during their one-off Japanese show, was eager to get his older brother's band back together for one last shot at trying to make an album the fans would be proud of. Derek, Nigel and David weren't sure, but decided to meet for a drink anyway. They were thirsty. During this reunion, Nigel mentioned that he had a song, 'Bitch School' that "was written with David in mind." Shrimpton dutifully organized everyone's Palm Pilot calendars and scheduled in a rehearsal to go through the song, "to see if they still had that Tap magic." Despite such a lengthy gap, the members slipped on their old Spandex costumes "which still fitted like a ribbed condom" and jammed around a few old numbers. Jeanine was present writing horoscopes,

TRACKLIST

1. 'Bitch School'
2. 'The Majesty of Rock'
3. 'Diva Fever'
4. 'Just Begin Again'
5. 'Cash On Delivery'
6. 'The Sun Never Sweats'
7. 'Rainy Day Sun'
8. 'Break Like the Wind'
9. 'Stinkin' Up The Great Outdoors'
10. 'Springtime'
11. 'Clam Caravan'
12. 'Christmas With the Devil'
13. 'Now Leaving On Track 13'
14. 'All The Way Home'

BREAK LIKE THE WIND TOUR

ACCESS NO AREAS
I'M ALLOWED
TO BE HERE!

as always, and Nigel did not acknowledge her presence. It was just like old times. Tap were back – and on a mission to sell-out more than ever before.

Break Like the Wind – unbelievably the band's seventeenth album – a title inspired by the flatulence issues of former manager Ian Faith – and released on their own label, Dead Faith, also a "tribute" to their ex-manager, prompted a six-week, twenty-one-city tour of the United States and England that began on May 17, 1992, at an Air Force base in Colorado Springs and culminated in a sell-out show on July 7 at London's Royal Albert Hall. *Break Like the Wind* included new tunes such as 'Bitch School' and 'Cash On Delivery' (with Derek on vocals), as well as protest songs (a genre the band had at one time vowed never to write) such as 'Stinking Up the Great Outdoors' and 'Now Leaving on Track 13,' Nigel's song about euthanasia. "What we're saying with this album is," declared Nigel, "we're back. Join us, won't you, in a consumer sense." Nigel sums up the album's importance succinctly (sort of): "To me, the whole record is like those little dolls that you take apart, and there's a little doll in it, and you take it apart, and there's another little doll. And the mystery of course, is if you could take the smallest doll apart, what would be inside it? Would there be another big one? That's really *Break Like the Wind* – a metaphor masked as a parable posing as an allegory."

It was during that tour of the United States and England that Tap had asked their tour promoter, *What A Comotion! Promotions*, to produce a new stage prop. They had originally asked for a giant coffin lid to dangle above the entire audience that was lowered by a few metres at the beginning of each song to increase the sense of claustrophobia caused by the songs, but for Health and Safety reasons (all the rage in the '90s), this idea was nixed. Instead, the band were given "Jim," a giant skull that had been the leftover from a horror movie spin-off from the franchise *Honey I Shrunk the Kids* (1989), itself a horror movie of sorts. "Jim" was fitted with a smoke machine inside (it was a fogger's job to blow smoke out of "Jim's" bottom) along with two reflector lamps to make his eye sockets light up. Pleased at "Jim's" overall size and dimensions – following Faith's 'Stonehenge' screw-up in 1982 – the band had but one request for "Jim." They wanted to finish their set with 'Big Bottom' and could think of now greater ending to their concerts than "Jim" spinning around to reveal a woman's bottom, complete with garter belt and tattoos. The band got their wish and "Jim" became the fourth official member of the band in summer of 1982, much to the annoyance of Ric Shrimpton who, despite lovingly bringing the band back together in honour of his dead older brother (by 20 minutes), was not deemed worthy to be an official member of the group.

- PLATTER OF BLUE CHEESE
- PLATTER OF SOFT CHEESE
- PLATTER OF CHEDDAR CHEESE
- 135 MINI ROLLS
- 1 BOTTLE OF WATER

Opposite: *Back together for the first time. Again.*
Above: *Band rider, 1994.*

"We are such fans of your music and all of your records ... I'm not speaking of yours personally, but the whole genre of the rock 'n' roll."

Lt. Hookstratten

"OUR LYRICS HAVE MATURED SINCE 'SEX FARM.' HOW FAR? IT'S THE DISTANCE FROM A FARM TO A SCHOOL. MAN IS BORN ON THE FARM ... AND THEN HE GOES TO SCHOOL."

DEREK SMALLS

Album Reviews

Intravenus de Milo
Spinal Tap

"This tasteless cover is a good indication of the lack of musical invention within. The musical growth rate of this band cannot even be charted. They are treading water in a sea of retarded sexuality and bad poetry."

• The Gospel According to Spinal Tap
Spinal Tap

"This pretentious ponderous collection of religious rock psalms is enough to prompt the question: What day did the Lord create Spinal Tap and couldn't he have rested on that day too?"

WE ARE ALL FLOWER PEOPLE (1968)
SPINAL TAP

"Megaphone's stupidest, and least successful, record release of 1968 is a funny-not-funny concept album based on the misadventures of Icarus. Why Icarus deserves such treatment is never outlined, but the poor guy must be spinning in his grave after listening to this. Alas, rather than soaring, this album nose-dives straight into the sun, thankfully burning up instanteously like the hot mess that it is."

SHARK SANDWICH
SPINAL TAP

"Shit Sandwich"

Jap Habit (1975)
Spinal Tap

"What on earth were they thinking?"

Brainhammer (1970)
SPINAL TAP

"It may only be 23 minutes long, over ten tracks, but this dirge of immature metal mixed with pretend pop hooks, featuring the single 'Big Bottom,' feels like it goes on for an eternity. Acne-ridden teenage boys will salivate (and something else!) over the overwrought use of sexual imagery, dreadful puns and bad metaphors. Everyone else will stay clear for fear of catching any and all venereal diseases that seep from the pungent holes of every track on the album."

Spinal Tap Sings "(Listen to the) Flower People" and Other Favourites (1967)

"The British Invasion continues to beat to death the eardrums of the so-called 'teenager' movement, who continue to lap up this stream of happy-clappy flower-power drivel. Songs like 'Have a Nice Death' and 'Oh Dear, Oh Dear' will have you welcoming tinnitus with open arms ... and ears."

The Sun Never Sweats (1975) – SPINAL TAP
"With 'Daze of Knights of Old' as the standout track, i.e. the first one, *The Sun Never Sweats* is littered with bad puns, worse melodies, and some of the most hideous guitar solos ever performed on record. The band's loud guitarist, Nigel Tufnel, has done the impossible: made being a guitar player in a rock 'n' roll band look as uncool as working as a manager at a leisure centre in Basildon."

"We've never been a critics' band."

Derek Smalls

TAP UP CLOSE:
NIGEL TUFNEL

Guitarist. Lead guitarist. Gumby-enthusiast. *Car and Driver* **reader. Oreo obsessive. Nigel Tufnel is all those things and, perhaps, even more. Between 1967 and 1984, Tufnel and the rest of the Tap, would have no idea – literally no clue – that their music would have no impact on the world of rock 'n' roll at all.**

Born to humble and ever-so slightly dingy beginnings in East London's Squatney in 1947, Nigel Tufnel would be the first to admit that his formative years at school were incredibly rock 'n' roll. But, sadly, just in the sense that the only toys his family could afford for him to play with were a rock and a bread roll that his mother, Nigella Tufnel gave him every morning before sending him on his way to St Scubbins' Primary School, a stone's throw away from his family's one-up, one-down, three-across, 1920s-build council house. Home life for Nigel was tough. His family, in particular his mother, were distinctly unmusical and saw the burgeoning Liverpudlian skiffle-group scene that Nigel was beginning to be influenced by as a complete waste of time. "Just awful," is how Nigel's mother would describe these bands, often quite rightly.

If no one at home understood Nigel and his new love of major chords A through G, life at school was even tougher. He had trouble concentrating and would constantly be sent to detention for looking outside the classroom window, appearing to be staring vacantly at nothing, an activity he was most content to do for most of the day, to the detriment to his education. From the age of four until he was six, Nigel would get into trouble, even if he rarely understood why and how. His school report at the age of five went into great detail – an uncommon practice at that age – about Nigel's inability to grasp rudimentary curriculum subjects, but explained how he did have a wide understanding and fondness for creative arts, such as haberdashery and music. Even his teacher, Miss Morland, was stunned that he could play all the chords on a guitar, including the jazzy one, F# minor diminished, but he was not able to recite past J on the alphabet.

After showing an inclination towards "the devil's music," Nigel was given his first guitar by his father, a Sunburst "Rhythm King" Fender Telecaster, when he was six. His father gave in to Nigel's diva-like tantrums to buy him the guitar after he became worried about his child's "life choices" when he caught Nigel "masturbating" a tennis racquet in front of a mirror while

"I'm really influenced by Mozart and Bach."

Nigel Tufnel

Above: *Nigel, with David and Derek.*

Opposite: *Just Nigel.*

dressed in his mother's tights and favourite blouse. If it wasn't for the Tufnels' neighbour and St Scubbins' school friend David St Hubbins, Nigel's career in music may have never blossomed at all. David, the boy next door, whose family were more progressive and allowed their child to listen to blues-jazz and jazz-blues (between the hours of 3–5pm on Saturdays only) and folk music. It was David's music, blaring out of his bedroom window, that turned Nigel on to the sounds of early pop and R&B. The two became firm friends and would spend their afternoons after school sitting on their beds singing the

songs of Honkin' Bubba Fulton, Little Sassy Francis and Big Little Daddy Coleman (a deaf guitar player), music they heard on a neighbour's radio. Fusing all their early blues-jazz and jazz-blues influences, David and Nigel wrote their first song, a ballad in D, called "All the Way Home." The song would inspire the two boys to run home from school everyday (even on weekends) and lock themselves away in their bedrooms. Both boys' parents considered this activity to be very strange and unhealthy even though it was the '60s and every boy in the country was trying to be the next Lennon and/or McCartney.

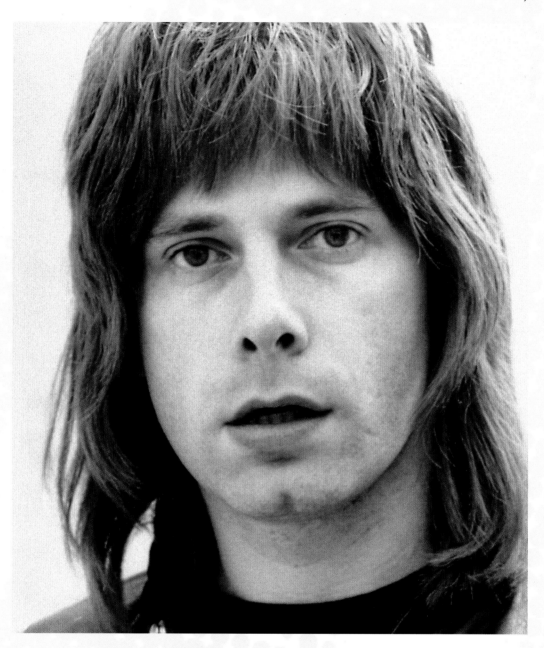

"If I couldn't be a rock star,
I suppose I could work in a shop
of some kind, or do freelance,
selling some sort of product,
you know..."

Nigel Tufnel

THOSE THAT WERE THERE: IAN FAITH

Ian Faith's downfall as Spinal Tap's incompetent manager reached its bottom-most rung when he made too much of a little thing out of a thing that should have been big, i.e. the 'Stonehenge' scenery. But that wasn't all. He quit the band amid a series of embarrassing tantrums, behaviour that allowed the rise to power of Tap's ambitious tambourine player, Jeanine Pettibone.

"I am the fifth member of Spinal Tap, after all. Their Pete Best, Brian Epstein, George Martin and Murray the K all wrapped in one."

Ian Faith

"It's not your job to be as confused as Nigel is."

David St Hubbins to Ian Faith

Despite a body, a coffin and an actual funeral, rumours of Ian Faith's "death" in 1990, were greatly exaggerated. His "death" however was the catalyst that Derek, David and Nigel required after six years of rock 'n' roll exile (a fate worse than telesales) following the home video success of Marty DiBergi's *This Is Spinal Tap*. It was Ian Faith who had allowed DiBergi into the band's inner sanctum, with no contractual paperwork, to allow the band the rather basic right to approve final cut of the film, as well as increasingly becoming a pushover over the *Smell the Glove* album artwork "debacle," the cancellation of shows during the 1982 tour and the "King Leisure bed" farce that arose in Memphis, Tennessee, following a hotel room cock-up. Ian's incompetence had become too much to bear for the band, a situation that reached its nadir during the 1982 U.S. tour when the increasingly pressurized manager was asked to supply details to Texan artist, Polly Deutsch, for a life-size replica of Stonehenge, scenery that the band hoped would revive their lagging stage presence. Despite Nigel supplying Ian with the incorrect specifications required, given to her on a napkin sketch drawn by Nigel, the resulting foam artwork was 18 inches high instead of 18 feet, a complication that arose incomprehensibly from the respective metric/imperial systems of Britain and America. "Whether Nigel knows the difference between feet and inches is not my problem. I do what I'm told," Ian retaliated.

Deutsch's insistence that she was only following Ian's orders, prompted the visibly frustrated manager to claim "It's my job to do what I'm asked to do by the creative element of this band," and "Fuck the napkin!"

Not a band to waste good foam, or dwarfs, the group used the mini-monolith onstage during the next show in Austin, Texas, where small people had been hired to salvage the situation and dance around the scenery giving a sense of false perspective to those in the audience. Despite the dwarfs, David was not impressed: "I do not, for one, think that the problem was that the band was down. I think that the problem may have been that there was a Stonehenge monument on the stage that was in danger of being crushed by a dwarf. Alright? That tended to understate the hugeness of the object."

This debacle prompted the departure of Ian as Tap's once-devoted manager, and the downward spiral of the *Smell the Glove* album, which concluded with Nigel walking out on the band too. It was Nigel's last contact with Ian that prompted the now ex-manager to secure one final tour for the band, following the No.5 success of 'Sex Farm' in the Japanese charts.

While the band never heard or saw Ian again – except for stamping dirt into his "grave" – the Japanese tour breathed life back into the band (except Mick Shrimpton, who died) one last time before their extended hiatus until 1992.

Despite his inability to manage bands, Ian Faith remained a band manager after parting ways with Spinal Tap, forming the management co-operative the Managing Wilburys, a consortium of managers "who travel around giving career advice to bands who would stay in the same place."

Opposite: *Second from left – Ian.*

"In the topsy, turvy world of heavy rock, having a good solid piece of wood in your hand is quite often useful."

Ian Faith

"MY GUITAR SOLOS ARE MY TRADEMARK."

NIGEL TUFNEL

FORMER BAND MEMBERS

From 1964 to today, there have been many (too many?) band members who have come and gone. Some have died, some have survived, some have even thrived, but what connects them all is that all of them have lived. And been in Spinal Tap. What follows is a comprehensive collection of players and shakers who made an impact on Spinal Tap's long (too long?) career and were excellent scapegoats for Derek, Nigel and David when the going got tough.

The issue of Spinal Tap's spiralling addiction to hiring and firing, and killing off, band members had only infrequently been discussed by Derek, Nigel, and David before Marty DiBergi's documentary delved deeper. Being British, the principal trio had always tried to sweep the subject under the proverbial rug, not wanting to confront their demons despite being well-known Satanists and fans of the occult. "You've got to understand that in the world of rock 'n' roll there are certain changes that sometimes occur, and you've just got to, sort of, roll with them," David told DiBergi, when the director quizzed the singer over the departure of guitarist Nigel, a few hours earlier. "I mean you saw exactly how many people who's been in the band over the years, 37 people's been in this band over the years. It's like, you know, six months from now, I can't see myself missing Nigel more than I might miss Ross MacLochness, or Ronnie Pudding, or Denny Upham, or "Little" Danny Schindler, or any of those, you know."

From short-term hires, whose names may have been washed away by history, to major players whose names are etched in Tap's history book (more of a tome), the sheer volume of former members paints a picture of how difficult it must be to be in Spinal Tap. To those who have survived, and continue to rock, we salute you. To those who are dead, how are you reading this?

While David informed DiBergi during *This Is Spinal Tap* that there had been 37 people in the band, it appears David was ill-informed of his own band's history. After the group invited me to write this book, I asked my unpaid intern to research the real number while I ran other errands. My intern, in turn, farmed it out to some guy called "Wicky," and it appears that only 20 former band members have been documented. Let's start there. My publisher only allowed me to have three pages, so apologies to anyone who didn't make the cut, I didn't think you were important enough.

"LITTLE" DANNY SCHINDLER

The American vocalist and harmonica player (harmonicayer?), "Little" Danny Schindler played in David and Nigel's pre-Tap bands the Thamesmen, the Originals, et al, for the turbulent 18 months throughout 1965-66. Bored of playing second fiddle to David and Nigel's many merry tunes, "Little" Danny left to front his own band, the Shvegman-Hayman-Kvelkman Blues Band Featuring Little Danny Schindler, despite being unable to sing. In the 1980s, "Little" Danny became more formally known as "Little" Daniel when he became a successful record executive.

LHASA APSO

A back-up vocalist who performed with David/Nigel in their respective bands during the 18-month period in 1965–66, before Nigel and David came together. Lhasa was the girlfriend of Thamesmen bassist Ronnie Pudding. When they split up, Lhasa later dated David, who made her immortal when her bum became the inspiration for 'Big Bottom.' A sizeable contribution to the early success of Tap in 1970.

FORMER MEMBERS LIST

ADAMS, JIMMY (horn) 1965–66
APSO, LHASA (vocals) 1965–66
BESSER, JOE "MAMA" (drums) 1982
BOND, PETER "JAMES" (drums) 1974–77
BRIXTON, TONY (keyboards) 1965–66
CHILDS, ERIC "STUMPY JOE" (drums) 1969–74
CLOVINGTON, GEOFF (horn) 1965–66
FLEETWOOD, MICK (drums) 1998–
LAINE, DICKY (keyboards) 1965–66
MACLOCHNESS, ROSS (keyboards), 1974–75
PEPYS, JOHN "STUMPY" (drums) 1964–69
PETTIBONE, JEANINE (tambourine), 1982
PUDDING, RONNIE (bass), 1966–67
SCHINDLER, "LITTLE" DANNY
  (harmonica, vocals), 1965–66
SCRUBBS-MARTIN, JULIE (vocals), 1965–66
SHRIMPTON, RIC (drums), 1992–99
SKUFFLETON, SKIPPY (drums) 2000–
UPHAM, DENNY (keyboards), 1966–68
VAN DER KVELK, JAN (keyboards), 1965
VANSTON, C.J. (keyboards), 1992–
WAX, NICK (keyboards), 1965–66

JOE "MAMA" BESSER

Seen playing the drums at the end of DiBergi's *This Is Spinal Tap*, Joe "Mama" Besser was officially announced as Tap's fattest member when he played drums during the band's one-date tour at Kobe Hall, Japan to support the 1982 album *Smell the Glove*, following Mick Shrimpton's onstage explosion. Oddly, Joe was never seen again after the gig. It's safe to assume he's dead.

PETER "JAMES" BOND

Born and living between 1949 and 1977, Tap's third drummer, Peter "James" Bond was the curly-haired drummer who replaced Eric "Stumpy Joe" Childs in 1974, shortly before the release of the concept album, *The Sun Never Sweats*. A snappy dresser and ultimate professional, Bond spontaneously combusted while performing with his side-band Buddahead at the Isle of Lucy Blues-Jazz / Jazz-Blues Festival. Many audience members believed his death was part of the show and were horrified when they heard the truth, which had to be broadcasted out of the festival's loudspeakers, a legal requirement to downplay any rumours of wrongdoing on the organizers' behalf. Though Nigel did announce the specifics of his death in Dibergi's documentary: "He just was like a flash of green light, and that was it. Nothing was left. Well, there was a little green globule on his drum seat. It was a small stain, actually."

ERIC "STUMPY JOE" CHILDS

Born in 1945, the former Wool Cave drummer "Stumpy Joe" was invited to become Tap's second drummer in 1969 after John "Stumpy" Pepys died (was murdered?) in "a bizarre gardening accident." A session drummer, "Stumpy Joe" played on 1967's '(Listen to the) Flower People and its B-side 'Rainy Day Sun' and joined the group officially in 1969. "Stumpy Joe" performed on four of Tap's least profitable albums before succumbing to the Tap Curse. He choked to death (on someone else's vomit) in 1974. The owner of the vomit is still at large. "They can't prove whose vomit it was. They don't have the facilities in Scotland Yard," Nigel concluded on the subject.

ROSS MACLOCHNESS

Joining Tap as keyboardist in 1974, just before for the release of the concept album, *The Sun Never Sweats*, the former Kilt Kids member with an incredibly fast left hand ultimately blamed for the album's whelming – the album was overwhelming, the sales were underwhelming, leaving it evenly scored at simply 'whelming' – critical and commercial response. With Viv Savage sitting in his seat by 1975, Ross retired from music to pursue missionary work in Namibia.

JOHN "STUMPY" PEPYS

The group's first official drummer, John "Stumpy" Pepys, "the Peeper," was a tall, blond geek of a man, who often reminded David of the actor Ed Begley Jr. Given his own stool to sit on in 1964, "Stumpy" met future Tappers David and Nigel when they performed together in the Johnny Goodshow Revue. These three warriors of acoustic folk, formed Spinal Tap together, with the appointment of bassist Ronnie Pudding and keyboardist Denny Upham in December 1966, when they played their first gig at London's Music Membrane. "the Peeper" died (was murdered?) in a bizarre gardening accident immediately after the band released their first live album, *Silent But Deadly*. Nigel recalled: "It was really one of those things the authorities said, 'Well, best leave it unsolved.'"

RIC SHRIMPTON

Mick Shrimpton's twin brother (younger by 20 minutes), Ric, occupied his brother's Tap shoes from 1992 to 1999. Cutting his teeth, like his older brother (by 20 minutes) as the house drummer for the Eurovision Song Contest, it was Ric who got the band back together following their eight-year hiatus, after *Smell the Glove*. The band were originally sceptical of hiring Ric, claiming they had already broken his mother's heart once. They relented, and for the next seven years played like a band reformed. Because they had reformed. Ric played his first gig with the band on January 30, 1992. Local drummers were on call in case of any sudden death emergencies, and St John's Ambulance at the gig had been made aware of the situation. In 2000, Ric – "the nicest drummer we've ever had," said Nigel – was presumed dead.

Harriet Sternberg, Tap's manager and agent at the time, pulled the shortest straw out of a sock and had the daunting task of telling Mrs Shrimpton that her second son was likely to be the most recent, but least surprising, victim of the Curse.

DENNY UPHAM

Denny Upham, a strikingly handsome piano man whose right arm was considerably longer than his left – thus allowing him to play all 88 keys in one go – was the first keyboardist to perform with the newly formed Spinal Tap when the band played their first gig in December 1966, and was co-founder of the band, though he disliked the name Spinal Tap, preferring Silver Service, a name mooted at the time. Following the shocking reaction to the group's concept album, *We Are All Flower People*, Denny was dismissed; his use of particular keyboard sounds and the overall volume level was deemed the critical failing.

FRIEND OF THE BAND
STELLAZINE
LEAD SINGER OF THE DOSE

"Maybe there's two of them," Ian joked, when he heard about the Dose, the New-wave/punk band that opened for Spinal Tap during a leg of their 1982 US tour. It was lead singer, Stellazine, whose intimacy with David, Nigel, Derek, Viv and Jeanine spread the HSV-1 virus, rendering the lips of said faces with unsightly cold sores. Only Mick Shrimpton could refuse the temptations of Stellazine's infamous fuck-me boots.

"It's such a fine line
between stupid and clever."

David St Hubbins

TAPOGRAPHY

Even for a band who have been around as long as they have, Spinal Tap have still released *a lot* of stuff. Perhaps too much? Renowned for their punctuality as much as the prolificness, the group has always been of the mind that quantity trumps quality.

STUDIO ALBUMS

Spinal Tap Sings "(Listen to the) Flower People" and Other Favourites (1967)
We Are All Flower People (1968)
Brainhammer (1970)
Nerve Damage (1971)
Blood to Let (1972)
Intravenus de Milo (1974)
The Sun Never Sweats (1975)
Bent for the Rent (1976)
Tap Dancing (1976)
Rock 'n' Roll Creation (referred to as The Gospel According to Spinal Tap in the film) (1977)
Shark Sandwich (1980)
Smell the Glove (1982)

LIVE ALBUMS

Silent But Deadly (1969)
Jap Habit (1975)

COMPILATIONS

The Incredible Flight of Icarus P. Anybody (1969)
Heavy Metal Memories (1983)

SINGLES

'All the Way Home' (1961, unreleased demo)
'Gimme Some Money' (1965)
'(Listen to The) Flower People' (1967)
'Breakfast of Evil' (1969)
'Big Bottom' (1970)
'Swallow My Love' (1970)
'Nerve Damage' (1971)
'Blood to Let' (1972)
'Tonight I'm Gonna Rock You Tonight' (1974)
'Stonehenge' (1975)
'Nice 'N Stinky' (1975)
'Heavy Duty' (1976)
'Bent for the Rent' (1976)

'Tap Dancing' (1976)
'Rock 'n' Roll Creation' (1977)
'Sex Farm' (1980)
'No Place Like Nowhere' (1980)
'Hell Hole' (1982)

BOOTLEGS

Top Hit for Nows (1968)
Audible Death (1969)
Live at Budokan (1975)
Openfaced Mako (1980)
Got Thamesmen on Tap (unknown date)
Maximum Tap (unknown date)
It's a Dub World (unknown date)

UNRELEASED ALBUMS

Here's More Tap
Flak Packet
Lusty Lorry
SEXX! (Original Motion Picture Soundtrack)
Hernia
Nigel Tufnel's Trilogy in D minor, including 'Lick My Love Pump' (working title)
Saucy Jack, musical based on the life of Jack the Ripper

SOLO RELEASES

NIGEL TUFNEL

Nigel Tufnel's Clam Caravan (1979)
Pyramid Blue (unknown date)

DEREK SMALLS

It's a Smalls World (1978)

ROSS MACLOCHNESS

Doesn't Anybody Here Speak English? (unknown date)

THIS IS Spinäl Tap ™

"David. David. David. Wait, please, wait a minute. Have you any idea what it will cost to dress up the band as animals?"

Ian Faith

BIBLIOGRAPHY

No man is an island, especially when it comes to Spinal Tap. As with rock 'n' roll itself, we must gratefully acknowledge the giants whose broad shoulders we all stand on. The author and publisher of this book offer their humble thanks to the following people and corporations, for their inspiration.

This Is Spinal Tap, The Official Companion (Bloomsbury, 2000)

StudioCanal
The cast and crew of *This Is Spinal Tap*.

Christopher Guest – Michael McKean – Harry Shearer – Rob Reiner

This book is lovingly dedicated to *This Is Spinal Tap*, the greatest film ever made.

Author

Wallace Fairfax hails from Clitheroe, Lancaster, North England. Wallace was not only the first UK journalist to interview Spinal Tap after their triumphant first gig (as Spinal Tap) at London's Music Membrane in 1966, he was also the very first person to buy their debut album. You can ask him, if you don't believe him. He kept the receipt. In 1971, Spinal Tap invited Wallace to travel with them around the world to document their rise to the top. At somewhere around the middle, in 1972, Wallace left rock 'n' roll disappointment behind "for a proper job" (his wife's words). Since then, Wallace has remained Spinal Tap's greatest fan, hence why they asked him to write this book.